STADIUM CHASE

By Adam Faiers and Dan McCalla

ADAM FAIERS AND DAN McCALLA

Copyright © 2013 Adam Faiers and Dan McCalla.
All rights reserved.
ISBN: 1482723549 ISBN-13: 978-1482723540

All views expressed within this book are the personal views of Adam Faiers. They do not represent Milton Keynes Dons Football Club, the MK Dons Sport & Education Trust, the Redway School or any other organisation.

Fixture list reproduced with kind permission of Football DataCo Ltd.

CONTENTS

	Acknowledgments	4
	Forewords/About The Charities	6
	Fixture List	10
1	How Hard Can It Be?	11
2	The Easy One To Start	21
3	Which Way To Dean Court?	31
4	The Heel Of God	52
5	Riding To Nothing	71
6	From Yeovil To Auckland	88
7	Carlisle	102
8	The Never-Ending Winter	128
9	Why I Ride	142
10	The Final Stage	154
	Epilogue	164
	About The Authors	167

ACKNOWLEDGMENTS
This book would not have been possible without…

AF: Deep breath… the mighty MK Army, especially Margaret Faiers, Nicola Jenkins, Chris and Emma, Dan McCalla, Ross Gallacher, Tony Hawkins and John Taylor; the MK Dons Supporters Association: John Brockwell, Jules the website king, Dave Gaskell, John Samuel, Tom Stewart, Edan Thorpe, Rex Burton, Matt Barnes and the players of MKDSA FC; MK Dons Sport and Education Trust: Dennis Woolford, Karl White, Judy Hildreth and Darren Oldroyd; and MK Dons FC: John Cove, Andrew Cullen, Sarah Bowen, James Parkinson, Sarah Thompson, Paul Heald, Karl Robinson, Pete and Bobby Winkelman, Simon Crampton, Damien Doyle, Gayle Sharpe, Anne Smith, Antoni Fruncillo and Simone Corgan.

Chris Reading, for incredible support and friendship; Robert Quirke and Quirke Plumbing; Colin Berry and Fossil Watches; Terry Brooks and Brooks Engineering Aylesbury; BDL Hotels: Sarah Goldsbrough, Ramada Encore Derby, Holiday Inn Express Tamworth and Holiday Inn Express Leeds Armouries; Roger Mott and all the drivers at Motts Travel; Kevin of Kings Ferry Coaches; Jacqui Cullen and Doubletree by Hilton Milton Keynes; James Hildreth; Jessica Cooper of BBC *Look East*; Luke Ashmead of BBC Three Counties Radio; Toby Lock of the MK Citizen; Mark Chapman and Robbie Savage of *606*. Leighton Buzzard Road Cycling Club: Iain Holloway-McLean, Stuart Tilbrook, Craig and Rob Nelson, Jason Horn, Keith Sheehan and all the members and committee; Matt and the team at Chaineys Cycles; Julian Thrasher and ATG Training; Lorraine Hobbs and Rachel Farrow of the Redway School; Carl Sewell and SmashIt PR; Gary Cartwright; Russ Bray; Unicorn Darts.

STADIUM CHASE

And all the following members of the extended family we call football: Cheltenham Town; Swindon Town; Cambridge City; Ewan Dunlop and Crawley Town; Tranmere Rovers; Adrian Plimmer and Shrewsbury Town; Brentford; Charles Swallow, Andy the groundsman, Clare Bailey and Doncaster Rovers; Alastair and James Constantine and Notts County; Steve Phillips and Crewe Alexandra; Sheffield Wednesday; the Carlisle United stewards; Portsmouth; Sheffield United; Dave Toyn and Stevenage; Matt Hudson and Colchester United; Avril Spraggon and Northampton Town; the supporters and community trusts of Cheltenham Town, Swindon Town and Brentford; the fans of Walsall and Preston North End; and everyone in the Corner Flag Bar at Hartlepool United.

DM: Now that Adam's finished his Oscar acceptance speech... thanks to my mum and dad, for giving me the time and space in Spain to get this bloody thing finished; to Mark and Jeni Sanderson of Fusing Creativity, for cover artwork and just generally being thoroughly lovely people; to every dedicated MK Dons fan (especially those that travel away) for making this such a fantastic club to support; and above all to Adam himself, for being an engaging subject, a wonderful friend, and for driving me to Plymouth and back for a pre-season friendly.

FOREWORD
By John Cove, Chief Executive, MK Dons SET

I'm very fortunate to hold the role I do in this wonderful club, as it brings with it a range of experiences and opportunities that I believe can't be matched elsewhere. As part of my role, I field most of the enquiries about the weird, wonderful and sometimes inspiring ideas people have that they would like to carry out in partnership with us. Over the years these have ranged from firewalking on the pitch (the face of our groundsman Joe Aylett was priceless when I asked him about it!) to holding an assembly for a newly formed school that found itself with a new student body of over 2000 young people.

However, one of the most inspiring ideas emerged from a conversation with Adam Faiers when he said that he wanted to raise money for the Trust. We are always enormously grateful for everyone who raises money for us, volunteers with us or supports us in one of the myriad different ways one can support an organisation such as ours. It is vital for us that this is continued in these difficult financial times so that the delivery of service can be maintained. But as Adam told me about his fundraising plan, I was about to launch into thanking him when he said: '…and I'm going to do it by riding to every away match.'

Now as those that know me will attest, I'm not often lost for words. But my mind immediately started to try to work out the size of the task in front of him. Carlisle was hundreds of miles away and so far north you could get a nose bleed, whilst Yeovil was a long way down south. How would it work? My face must have been a similar picture to Joe's when I mentioned the firewalking. As I regained composure and chatted it through with him further, we thought that it would be a good idea if he raised money for another good cause at the same time.

I said I would canvass the football management team

to see whether they would like to nominate an organisation. Our First Team are very supportive of the work that we do in the community and Karl Robinson, the Dons' First Team manager, had recently visited the Redway School and was bowled over by its work. Karl's response was almost instantaneous and the Redway School became part of Adam's adventure.

This book is a wonderful account of the triumph of the human spirit over, at times, horrendous circumstances and I cannot speak glowingly enough of Adam's effort and generosity in completing this task and for being a real ambassador for the SET and its work. Thank you very much, Adam!

ABOUT MK DONS SET

Milton Keynes Dons Sport and Education Trust is a Charitable Company Limited by Guarantee (number 1123762) and an award-winning organisation.

The team that brought the football club to Milton Keynes always intended to develop a robust, innovative and sustainable community legacy. Each year over 50,000 adults and children benefit from its holiday courses, matchday clubs, study support, tackling obesity programmes, team coaching, mini soccer and multi-sports programmes. These are delivered in partnership with a range of agencies and organisations including Milton Keynes Council, NHS Milton Keynes, schools and junior football clubs.

The organisation has grown from one full-time employee with 15 part-time staff in 2004 to 27 full-time staff, 31 part-time staff and over 50 volunteers by June 2010. It tries to be a learning organisation by actively seeking out best practice amongst football clubs and other local, regional and national agencies and organisations, in order that its programmes set benchmarks for quality and service.

FOREWORD
By Ruth Sylvester, Head Teacher, Redway School

Every year, the Redway School receives offers of help from many people. For example, last year we had money raised through karate exhibitions, and people holding bucket collections at Christmas. We are grateful for every pound received because it means we can provide more care and more opportunities for our students.

The Redway School has forged a great link with MK Dons over the past years. Some of our students play in the team's Disability Football programmes. Many of the players have been into school, and we are delighted that Karl Robinson and Alan Smith have personally helped us out with fund-raising efforts.

The GetSET1000 project, through the hard work of Adam Faiers, his willing team of volunteers, and especially the army of fans from MK Dons and other clubs up and down the UK, has helped us raise valuable money for our playground. I can't begin to describe the benefits that this will bring our young people. Imagine for a moment, though, the warm sun beating on your back and a cool breeze on your face. For some of our young people, these sensations give them a sense of well-being that many of us take for granted.

The equipment we have is expensive. Really expensive. Your donations have helped us, and will continue to help us long into the future. For that, I can't thank you enough.

ABOUT THE REDWAY SCHOOL

The Redway School caters for children and young people who need dynamic, specialised care. It has one member of staff for every pupil on site and provides a stimulating, caring and safe environment. Given the challenges it faces, it celebrates every achievement.

The Redway School is maintained by the Milton Keynes local authority, catering for children between the ages of two and 19 with a wide range of learning difficulties. The school is located in Netherfield, close to both the city centre and Milton Keynes Hospital. Its specialist facilities include a MiLE room (multisensory interactive learning environment), dark room, soft play room, Optimusic room, reading room, Art and Design room with a kiln, music room, hall, conservatory, gym and a hydrotherapy pool with sensory equipment.

FIXTURE LIST

Milton Keynes Dons F.C. away games, 2012/2013

Date	Home team	Competition
Saturday Aug 11	Cheltenham Town	Capital One Cup
Tuesday Aug 21	AFC Bournemouth	League 1
Saturday Aug 25	Swindon Town	League 1
Tuesday Sep 4	Northampton Town	JP Trophy
Saturday Sep 8	Walsall	League 1
Saturday Sep 22	Bury	League 1
Tuesday Oct 2	Coventry City	League 1
Sunday Oct 14	Preston North End	League 1
Tuesday Oct 23	Crawley Town	League 1
Saturday Oct 27	Scunthorpe United	League 1
Friday Nov 2	Cambridge City	FA Cup
Friday Nov 16	Tranmere Rovers	League 1
Tuesday Nov 20	Shrewsbury Town	League 1
Saturday Dec 8	Brentford	League 1
Tuesday Jan 1	Notts County	League 1
Saturday Jan 5	Sheffield Wednesday	FA Cup
Saturday Jan 26	Queens Park Rangers	FA Cup
Tuesday Jan 29	Yeovil Town	League 1
Saturday Feb 9	Oldham Athletic	League 1
Tuesday Feb 12	Doncaster Rovers	League 1
Saturday Feb 23	Carlisle United	League 1
Tuesday Feb 26	Portsmouth	League 1
Saturday Mar 9	Sheffield United	League 1
Tuesday Mar 19	Crewe Alexandra	League 1
Saturday Mar 23	Colchester United	League 1
Friday Mar 29	Hartlepool United	League 1
Saturday Apr 13	Leyton Orient	League 1
Saturday Apr 27	Stevenage	League 1

CHAPTER 1: HOW HARD CAN IT BE?

When I was 15 years old, I realised that my calling in life was to win the Devizes to Westminster Canoe Race.

I came to this mildly bizarre conclusion when I first saw the race on the TV one Good Friday. I saw a band of heroic individuals paddle 125 miles along the Kennet and Avon Canal from Devizes to Reading, and then downstream along the Thames all the way to Westminster over four gruelling days. As if that wasn't enough, the route also contained 76 locks, where competitors had to get out of their canoes, carry them around on foot, and then get back in and carry on. To this day, I still have no idea why I decided to turn round to my parents and declare: "I'm going to win that."

Having moved to Belgium shortly after being born, and then moving on to Saudi Arabia, I really didn't have much of a clue about canoeing apart from a short course on the Grand Union Canal in Leighton Buzzard in the holidays one year. My parents moved around a lot for work, and they needed to keep me busy over the school holidays one year, during the brief periods that they were in the UK. My mum was a bit worried that I didn't do much exercise and I don't think she wanted me piling on the pounds. So she gave me a challenge: she said if I ran a marathon, she'd give me £100. But one thing I noticed about the long-distance canoeing was that all the competitors had support teams giving them sandwiches, cake and chocolate as they raced. Here was the best of both worlds, I thought. Not only would I get the money, but I could eat as much as I wanted. The ideal sort of challenge!

Having enjoyed the course so much, I spent the next few months saving up to buy a canoe. I joined the local club in Bedford, where I stayed during term-time, and my resolve to win the race quietly grew. You cannot imagine how disappointed I was when, at the age of 15, I travelled up to the annual Canoe and Kayak exhibition to enter the race the following February to find that I had to be 18 to enter the singles event. After an ice-cream, I decided that I only had three more years to wait, so I'd use that time to get a bit fitter.

Being at a boarding school in Bedford and not being particularly bright academically meant I'd developed a resilience and a bloody-mindedness that meant I was definitely going to win it eventually. I started racing properly, which meant racing every weekend. With parents abroad, it meant getting lifts off anyone and everyone I could find, which wasn't easy with a 17-foot canoe in tow, but it was great fun nonetheless. Although I couldn't enter the big race, I could do the preparation races: a series of seven that covered the entire 125-mile course. What followed was three years of the best fun I've ever had; freezing cold, mud, capsizing in stinking canals and making some really good friends. No amount of bad results, near-hypothermia or near-drownings (two) could put me off.

In 1992, at the age of 21, I did it. I became the youngest person at that time ever to win the Devizes to Westminster in the singles class. Not only that, I'd absolutely dominated the race, ending up with a final winning margin of about 25 minutes. The problem that was that my life's work was (apparently) complete. I didn't have a clue what to do next. Doing it all again seemed a bit pointless, and anyway, there were other, very different challenges on the way. I met Margaret at a local pub, The Three Locks when we were both working there. At first, a lanky bloke in lycra didn't appeal to her but after a year, we were living together. I held down a steady job and Izzie, our daughter, was born about a year later.

My six years prior to Izzie's birth had mostly been focused on canoeing, and sadly, an intimate knowledge of the River Thames and a BTEC National Diploma in Leisure Studies (yes, I know!) doesn't really get you too far in the world of work. After five years of working in a shop (albeit a very nice shop), I decided that to start earning some decent money, I would have to get a degree. So I went back to school, ironically in the same year that Izzie started school full-time, starting a BSc in Environmental Management at Cranfield University. With only Margaret working and my college fees to pay, we were so strapped for cash that we couldn't afford to run a car. So I started riding to and from my lectures by bike.

Having failed to satisfy my appetite for endurance events since I'd stopped canoeing, I revelled in the 13 miles each way that I had to ride between Leighton Buzzard and Cranfield every day. So it was no surprise that I quickly started to take more and more of an interest in cycling as a sport. After I graduated, I soon got a job in Towcester, the other side of Milton Keynes from Leighton Buzzard, which was 23 miles away and just about in range for me to keep cycling to work. And so I kept at it, pushing those pedals 46 miles every day in all weathers. I started to time myself to see just how quickly I could do it. You might be wondering how I coped with the maze of roundabouts that is Milton Keynes, but being more interested in going quickly, I used the A5 trunk road and just breezed past the lot of them. Even now, a decade on, I still consider my fastest time for the 23 miles of just 52 minutes as nothing short of impressive.

So now you know me, Adam Faiers the forty-something club cyclist. But you don't know Adam Faiers, the football fan, just yet. And I'm sure every single football fan reading this book is asking themselves: "How on earth did this guy end up supporting MK Dons, of all teams?"

As you may already know, the history concerning the formation of Milton Keynes Dons Football Club out of the ashes of the ailing and transplanted Wimbledon was controversial when it happened in 2004, and remains contentious today. After promising to build the club its own state-of-the-art stadium, a consortium led by Pete Winkelman convinced the Norwegian owners of the financially destitute Wimbledon to ship the club to Milton Keynes. The decision was referred to an independent FA panel, which voted in May 2002 to allow the then-proposed move (at which point disgruntled Wimbledon fans formed their own club, AFC Wimbledon, in protest).

Some 16 months later, in September 2003, Wimbledon finally moved up the M1, into a converted National Hockey Stadium as the promised new ground was still a long way from completion (it wouldn't be opened until 2007). By this point, the vast majority of Wimbledon fans had joined the AFC movement, and the paucity of gate receipts had hit the cash-strapped club even harder, leading to financial administration. Wimbledon played out the rest of the season in MK, selling star players to pay the bills, finishing bottom of Division One (which would be renamed the Championship that summer) and dropping into the new League One. Faced with liquidation over the 2004 close-season, Winkelman's consortium, inter:mk, had to step in to buy the club outright. Winkelman took the chairmanship he still holds to this day and the club was renamed Milton Keynes Dons, to reflect both its new home and the history of where it came from. Even now, ten years after the move, many football fans still detest the way MK Dons came into existence. I don't mind that, although I do think the occasional cry of 'boycott' is a bit daft.

I'm still regularly asked the same question by opposition fans at our away games: "Who did you support before MK Dons arrived?" I know many Dons fans who did indeed do what many consider to be the dishonourable thing and dumped their previous team for the League One outfit that had arrived on their doorsteps. Many others are still fans of Premier League teams, but come to watch the Dons because it's their local professional team and they just can't afford to go to White Hart Lane or Stamford Bridge these days.

As for me, despite a keen interest in football, I can honestly say that I never supported a club side prior to MK Dons. You may find that hard to believe of someone my age, but it's true. Being born in Luton, it's natural to assume that I'd support Luton Town. But I've never felt an affinity to them – either the club or the town itself. When I eventually moved back to Leighton Buzzard at the age of 19, I was always more attracted to shiny new MK, even though I lived roughly equidistant between Luton and Milton Keynes. Back then, the futuristic Point, the entertainment complex that housed the UK's first multiplex cinema, had just opened and it was part of what made me feel that Milton Keynes was the hip place to be. It also didn't help that the only way to get from Leighton Buzzard to Luton without a car was (and still is) by bus, and I always used to get travel-sick on buses.

Before MK Dons came about, I would have described myself as a 'casual football observer'. I always made an effort to watch and enjoy all the England games, but I just never had a reason to get 'hooked' onto a particular club. One of my brothers-in-law supports Oxford United and took me to their old stadium, the Manor Ground, now and again (never have I passively smoked more than on the

Manor's terraces). But Oxford wasn't my town. My other brother-in-law is a big Sheffield Wednesday supporter, and I had many a boozy day out with him as we went to watch the Owls play at Hillsborough, but the same problem applied. Even the fact that my grandfather was such a huge Arsenal fan that he had his ashes scattered at Highbury wasn't enough.

I have fond memories of Euro 96, of Michael Owen's goal against Argentina in the 1998 World Cup and, slightly strangely, of Liverpool beating Alaves 5-4 in that crazy UEFA Cup Final in 2001. But still nothing could sway me into backing one horse. That all started to change when Izzie started playing football for one of Leighton United's junior teams, going to training every week and playing games on Saturday mornings. Every so often, she was able to go and watch MK Dons on a cheap ticket, a promotion available to most local junior football clubs a couple of times each season. Many of the parents went with their children, too, but due to work commitments I was never able to make it.

That all changed in May 2008, when Izzie dragged me along to the final game of the season against Morecambe. It had been a very successful season for the Paul Ince-managed Dons, who had won the Johnstone's Paint Trophy at Wembley just over a month earlier and had just clinched the League Two title (and promotion back to League One) as well. Because Izzie had started going to more games, I'd been taking more of an interest in the Dons' results and had kept an eye on their success. I'd followed the early years of MK Dons just because it was of local interest and I could read about it in the local paper. At the time, I just thought: "Ooh, this is a bit different. I wonder if it'll work out." But there was no desire from me to go and see a game, and back then I didn't have the spare money to shell out for football tickets anyway.

But on that spring Saturday, along with a huge crowd of about 17,000 people at the new stadium:mk, I watched a relatively uninspiring match that finished 1-1, but after seeing the Dons team presented with the League Two trophy at the end of the game, I was enchanted. This was 'my' town, and I realised that this was 'my' club. Within days, I had a season ticket for the following campaign and within months I was on the coach for my first away game to Bristol Rovers. Five trophyless and promotion-less League One seasons later, I still can't quite put my finger on what induced me into finally nailing my colours to the Dons mast. But I have loved every minute of it.

It was and still is exciting being part of the growth of the team and the club in Milton Keynes. I wanted to get involved with some of the projects that the MK Dons Supporters Association (MKDSA) were running, so I joined up. At one meeting, I floated the idea of cycling to Carlisle to raise money for the Academy. The looks I got were more than strange, so I decided to put the idea back in the box for the time being. But that dream never fully died and laid dormant at the back of my mind.

Towards the end of the 2011/2012 season, the Dons were firmly in the race for promotion from League One against much more illustrious opposition (the likes of Charlton Athletic, Sheffield Wednesday, Sheffield United and Huddersfield Town). We all still hoped that the Dons could claim automatic promotion to the Championship by finishing first or second in League One, safe in the knowledge that if we failed, we'd still get a second chance via the play-offs contested by the next four teams in the final table.

I went along to a fans forum around this time where the Dons manager, Karl Robinson, was asked how he prepared his team for big, important games. He took me by surprise when he said in passing that funds were limited for training equipment. By that, I'd assumed he was referring to things like tracking systems for players, which measure how far they run in training sessions, but he went on to list some real basic gear, like those metal man-shaped dummies used for free-kick drills. I knew Winkelman ran a tight ship financially when it came to playing budgets and so on, but this seemed like penny-pinching on an epic scale to me. Whether that was actually a true story or Karl was just exaggerating to make a point, I'll probably never know.

A short time later, I started reading up about the MK Dons Sport and Education Trust (known colloquially as the SET), largely because I'd heard a lot about what is one of the biggest disability football operations in the country and I knew very little about it. A question started rolling around in my head: "If Karl can't afford to buy equipment for the fully-professional first team, then how the hell does the SET get by?" I really wanted to do something to help. It felt the right thing to do, and anyway, it gave me a great excuse to get out on my bike!

As a keen club cyclist, I regularly cycle 60 miles on a Sunday morning, and occasionally I put in another 40 miles on a Saturday morning before a Dons home game (if there's no housework). I started to look at just how far away the other teams in League One were, and it seemed many were around 100 miles away. Therefore, in my relatively simplistic mind, I thought it would be pretty straightforward to cycle to away games. I could sell it to the wife by telling her I'd therefore be home on Sundays rather than out on the bike!

Enthused by the general idea, I started to crunch the numbers. With some feverish Google mapping, I worked out the cycling distances for every team we could possibly face the following season, both in League One (in case we didn't get promoted) and in the Championship (in case we did). Armed with all that data, I decided to try and find the balance of what would be a decent physical challenge to me but that would also be realistically achievable. Initially I was only going to do one ride, so I looked at the ones that were furthest away: Carlisle, Hartlepool and Exeter. But that didn't really seem like enough to me. "Anyone can do one long bike ride," I thought. "That's not going to capture people's imaginations." So I looked at doing some more, and listed all the ones I could realistically manage. Promotion or no promotion, it was looking like a 2012/13 season consisting of 15 or 16 rides (out of 23 away league games). At a push, I thought I might just about be able to spin that out to 20. So I made the pledge that I would try to cycle to as many as I possibly could, with the ultimate super-duper aim of riding to 20 over the course of the campaign.

With the idea and the beneficiary lined up, I let the idea simmer as I waited to see if the Dons could clinch promotion. Having wound up fifth in the final table, we were paired with Huddersfield in a two-legged play-off to decide who would face either Sheffield United or Stevenage in the final at Wembley. We played the first leg at home, but against a dogged Huddersfield team spearheaded by League One top scorer Jordan Rhodes, the Dons crashed to a 2-0 defeat. With the second leg up in West Yorkshire three days later and a mountain to climb, things looked bleak. It seemed almost certain that we would lose a League One play-off semi-final for the third time in four years.

Over the intervening days, I got more and more fired up about cheering the Dons on to an amazing comeback, and on May 14, the day before the second leg, I turned to Twitter to broadcast my new-found intentions: "@MKDonsFC win tomorrow & I'll cycle 1000miles next year to away games to raise money for the SET and a charity you choose!! #COYD #Believe"

I didn't expect much of a response, mainly because I re-read the tweet to myself and realised how insane it must have sounded to anyone who read it. But later that day, I noticed that John Cove, a director of the club and the man in charge of the SET, had retweeted it, as had a number of other people. Then the official Dons account retweeted me too, so I realised that this must have grabbed more peoples' attention than I'd first thought.

Up at Huddersfield, Rhodes scored in the first half to make it 3-0 on aggregate, and it looked like that was that. Then Daniel Powell got one back for us after half-time, and when former England and Manchester United striker Alan Smith nodded one in on 93 minutes, the Dons away end erupted in celebration. One more goal to get to extra-time! We can still do it!

Of course, we didn't. By the time Smith scored, the Huddersfield fans were already lining up for a pitch invasion, which duly ensued the moment the final whistle rang around the Galpharm Stadium about a minute later. We'd won the battle 2-1, but lost the war 3-2 on aggregate. While Huddersfield would go on to Wembley and clinch promotion (after a 22-kick penalty shoot-out against Sheffield United that went right down to the goalkeepers!), our season had ended. In disappointment. Again.

In the car on the way back down, however, I felt upbeat. I said I'd cycle to all those games if we won, and although we'd lost on aggregate, we'd won on the night. So I pledged at that point to stick to my promise and go for the challenge once the new season started in August. Besides, I was looking forward to it. After all, in the words of Jeremy Clarkson... "How hard can it be?"

CHAPTER 2: THE EASY ONE TO START

It was a good job that I'd been married to Margaret for 20 years already and knows me inside-out, because otherwise she'd have probably tried to get me sectioned when I first suggested riding to every away game.

She was used to me pushing myself to the limits and beyond in the name of endurance. I did a bit of long-distance running at one point, even doing a couple of 100-mile events. All she did was tell me that if my legs hurt afterwards, it was my own fault! So she took the idea of my project in her stride, although I don't think either of us really knew at that point what I (we) were letting myself (ourselves) in for.

From my initial promise to undertake this challenge, there was a period of around three months until the new season started in mid-August and I was going to have to start training. Over the course of that summer, the planning and the buzz around my project slowly grew and grew. One of the first things I did was to bring up the idea (again) at an MKDSA committee meeting, just to see what they thought and to see if they had any advice or tips. That meeting proved remarkably fruitful as one of my fellow members, Sarah Goldsbrough, was able to talk to her employers at BDL Hotels and got them to donate some free rooms for any long rides would take me more than one day, such as Bury, Preston, Hartlepool and Carlisle.

That development meant that some of the real long-haul games that were previously looking as if they were out of my reach suddenly became feasible. When the fixtures for the 2012/2013 season were released in mid-June, I was able to plan ahead for those longer games, go back to Sarah and tell her where I needed to stay and when. Thanks to help like this, the possibility suddenly opened up of being able to do every game.

In between all these happenings, I'd adopted a second beneficiary for the project. I'd spoken to John Cove, who'd told me that the SET disability programme would mainly be using the money raised to buy some much-needed tracksuits. To raise the profile a bit more, I offered to raise money for a fund of the first team's choice as well, and they collectively nominated the Redway School. At first, I didn't know about the school but it turns out that the Milton Keynes facility for highly dependent children was very close to the team's heart (Alan Smith, among others, had visited the school and met some of the pupils there). It was a wholly appropriate choice, and I felt it gave the whole endeavour an extra bit of gravitas. No longer was I just some chancer riding around on a wing and a prayer - there were two very important groups of people that I could really help.

I got the official confirmation of my hotel rooms on August 9, two days before our first competitive game of the season, away at Cheltenham Town in the League Cup. That day, I'd held a launch for my rides with Cove's help at an SET training session for the disability team. The attendance for it was remarkable, including the Mayor of Milton Keynes, Councillor Catriona Morris, who had separately chosen the SET as her official charity for her year-long tenure. As well as her, Cove and Winkelman both came along, as did both Dons first-team goalkeepers, David Martin and Ian McLoughlin, and their goalkeeping coach Paul Heald. Robinson wasn't there, which meant I actually got to do a reasonable amount of talking, but the launch wasn't as successful as I'd hoped. It didn't really gain the attention of any media outlets and to the local papers didn't really want to know. I don't think they were taking it or me seriously at that point.

That evening I was the guest on the MK Dons Radio Show, a weekly fan-run programme on a local station presented by three good friends of mine, Tony, John and Ross. This meant I could use the show to make the announcement that I was planning to do the full set of League One away trips. As I was driving to the studio, I realised that I was about to make a major balls-up. As our first away game was that League Cup game at Cheltenham, I was going to look pretty silly saying: "I'm riding to every game this season. Er, apart from the first one this Saturday. Sorry, folks. I don't do Cup games." I couldn't let the momentum falter by missing that first game out, so took the decision to include all our away games in the three Cup competitions as well as the 23 League away fixtures. I was sure Margaret wouldn't mind, despite my fate of destination being in the hands of the balls in the draw pot (or those silly playing cards they use on Soccer AM to do the Johnstone's Paint Trophy draw). Depending on the team's form, I might have to ride to one extra game, or in the worst case, as many as ten more!

My initial fears about a clumsy idea being presented on the radio show turned out to be groundless. I wasn't the only guest on the show, as Robinson had agreed to come along as well. Karl duly proceeded to spend 58 and a half minutes of a 60-minute show talking without pause, delivering a monologue that ranged from transfer targets to where he went on his summer holiday. I know Liverpudlians like to talk, but he clearly has two sets of lungs and it was truly something to behold. Once he finally paused for breath, I got 90 seconds to quickly explain who I was and what I was doing, followed by a couple of quips about how crazy I was, and then that was it.

Amongst all this, I had to focus on the first few games that lay ahead, and spent many an evening slaving away at my computer carefully planning out my routes. For the first few rides, I relied on handwritten notes for guidance, although it wasn't long before I began to hanker after a decent electronic bike computer with maps. Later in the season, a clubmate lent me a fantastic Garmin system with electronic maps loaded. It fitted to my handlebars and I would no longer get too waylaid or take the wrong turn (which happened a fair bit in the early stages of the season!)

A lot of thinking went into the roads I chose. For obvious reasons, I wanted to avoid major A-roads wherever possible to keep away from heavy traffic (and of course, motorways were out of the question!). This meant that many of my routes were made up of an intricate path of country roads, hopping from village to village like an old-fashioned steeplechaser. I also had to take climbing into consideration; there was no point scheduling a route ten miles shorter if it involved several hundred metres of extra uphill slogs. Obviously I was going to have to do some climbing – we don't live in Holland, after all – but the more I could minimise it, the better it would be for me. Chris Froome, I am most definitely not.

Along with all this planning came a heightened training regime, even though I was hardly out of practice on the bike to start with. As a matter of course, I would clock up 80 miles per week commuting and I'd also do another 60 miles at the weekend on a longer leisure ride. But it didn't take a genius to work out that even 140 miles every week wouldn't be enough, given that over the course of the season I'd regularly be doing single rides longer than that.

My cycling mates didn't really seem to appreciate the enormity of what I was doing at first, either. As the summer progressed, I found myself with fewer and fewer training partners as more of them felt like the distances I was preparing myself for were too much for them. Eventually, when I kept going out for rides on my own, they began to realise how seriously I was taking it.

I started taking longer, more winding routes to work, and I started doing leisure rides on both Saturdays and Sundays, easing my weekly mileage up towards the 200 mark. The aim I'd set myself was to be able to do 100 miles in a single outing by the time of the first away game. I'd managed that in the past, but many years previously, and I'd found more recently that 60 miles was pretty much my limit. And for someone over 40, it wasn't going to be easy to get myself well above and beyond that. But I dragged my way up towards it, and by the time the Cheltenham game came around, I was ready to go.

Much to my wife's annoyance, I'd already upgraded my bike. Although I already had a decent road bike, its many years of use were showing. And then a chance encounter in Chaineys Cycles (Shenley Church End, Milton Keynes – ask for Matt) changed my world. For me, the smell of a bike shop gets me going, and this particular day Chaineys seemed like Willy Wonka's factory would seem to Augustus Gloop after you' deliberately starved him for a fortnight. I clapped eyes on a new Giant TCR Advanced. It was a work of art. Ignoring the hefty price tag and dribbling from both sides of my mouth at the single piece of carbon, I innocently asked if I could sit on it. Just for a minute. I was still smiling three hours later when I got home and asked how we were doing for money that month...

Matt had offered me a very generous discount on it, so I thought that would be the best angle to use on Margaret: "It's just that I've seen a really nice bike... and I can get £900 off it!" She's known me long enough to know that if I want something that badly, my mind isn't going to be diverted from it, so we sat down, worked out if we could afford it, and managed to find the money to get it. It really is a one-off. Until the next one, I can't imagine I'm going to spend that kind of money on a bicycle ever again, especially as I'd probably have to factor the divorce settlement into the costs.

Having bought the carbon-framed wonder in February, I couldn't bear the thought of riding it out in the cold, getting it dirty and muddy, and potentially getting its carbon weave damaged by road salt. So I kept using my trusty older bike, leaving the new one in the kitchen, perfectly polished, with me sat at the kitchen table staring lovingly at it as if I were 14 years old again and sitting next to the best-looking girl at school.

Given the amount of money it cost, the lack of miles being notched up by the Giant's ornate wheels was starting to grate on Margaret. That in turn was making me feel guilty that I'd spent all that money. This led to the extra motivation I needed to crack on with this project – getting good, worthwhile use out of the Giant and keeping the wife off my back!

Looking back, that first ride to Cheltenham on August 11 seems bizarre. It was 65 miles on a glorious summer Saturday, which in the context of the whole season, was a fairly simple exercise. But at the time, it felt like some sort of epic. I was at the stadium preparing to start that morning when I bumped into Alan Smith in reception. Alan was (and is) someone I admire hugely. Having played for Leeds, Manchester United and Newcastle, as well as earning 19 caps for England, his career had hit the rocks after suffering a badly broken leg while playing for Man Utd against Liverpool in 2006.

After almost three years where he'd barely played a game, he'd joined the Dons the previous January on loan from Newcastle, and his dogged determination and penchant for 'getting stuck in' had made him a real favourite in my eyes. Scoring the winner against Sheffield United in April at stadium:mk, celebrating in front of 6500 travelling Blades fans and denying them a promotion party only reinforced that status. As did the end of the play-off game at Huddersfield, when a bunch of Terriers fans tried to confront him on the pitch and he resolutely stood his ground. They breed 'em tough in Leeds.

At the end of the 2011/2012 season, his Newcastle contract had expired, but he'd liked what he'd seen at the Dons so much that he signed a two-year permanent contract for us, believed to be worth around five per cent of the wage he was on at St James' Park. So it was fantastic for me to hear his words of encouragement before I left for the Cotswolds, although I was given a dose of reality when he turned to a friend and said: "He's picked an easy one to start, hasn't he?" To be honest, I was already nervous about the trip as it was, and Alan's off-hand comment didn't exactly help. "What if I break down? What if I get a puncture? What if I get lost?" I thought. And a 65-miler was supposed to be one of the easy ones?!

What helped me forget all of that stuff was my being inspired by all the achievements of British cyclists at the Olympics in London. The Cheltenham ride took place on the final weekend of the games, with Team GB's stars on two wheels having already brought in enough precious metal to fill Elizabeth Taylor's trinket box. That had lifted my spirits, with interest in cycling at an all-time high, and the words of encouragement I got from some of the other players as I departed at 9:30am (the same time as the team coach) helped.

After a bit of fun trying to race the coach over the first few miles, and a bit of banter from the coach driver, who knew of my project, I quickly settled into a rhythm. It was a gorgeous day, I had a tail-wind blowing me along, and the first few places on the route sped by. Out on the A421 to Buckingham, skirting around the north of Bicester to Aynho, it was then past Chipping Norton, across to Stow-on-the-Wold and then south-west into Cheltenham. This route meant I stayed well clear of Oxford and avoided the busy A40, which I only picked up for the last few downhill miles into Cheltenham itself.

Despite the lovely conditions and the relatively tranquil route, it was far from an easy ride. There was an unexpectedly large amount of climbing, because I hadn't appreciated how hilly the Cotswolds were going to be. Compared to the Chiltern Hills where I usually cycle, it was like trying to ride up an Alp while giving someone a backie. I plugged away at it, and by the time I reached the outskirts of Cheltenham, I found I was running surprisingly early. I rang Margaret, who was driving to the game with our friend Nicola, and found that they'd only reached Oxford and were still a good 45 minutes away from reaching me. So I sat on the side of the A40 outside town waiting for them to arrive. I would have carried on, but they had my change of clothes and my lunch! After a while, they arrived so I put by MKDSA top on and we raced each other through Cheltenham. Clearly bikes are faster than cars and I got to the ground first. Who needs 2.0 litres and fuel injection?

As I reached Cheltenham's Whaddon Road ground, and as I came past the Dons supporters coaches, none of the fans aboard really acknowledged my arrival. I guess none of them knew who I was or what I was doing. As I pulled into the car park, I was met by Robert Quirke, who had helped me out with some of the initial costs, the legend that is Dons goalkeeping coach Paul Heald, MKDSA treasure John Samuel, as well as Sam, a Dons fan who plays for one of the SET teams.

I also met Clive Gowing, the chair of the Cheltenham Town Supporters Society, who found me somewhere to get changed in the stadium before I headed into the supporters bar for a well-earned pint before kick-off. In the bar, I was greeted by all my friends, such as the guys from the radio show, and Dan (the man helping me write this book). I felt the reaction I got from them was warm, but they still didn't think I was going to do all the games.

Not because they thought I was full of myself (or something else) but simply because they thought I was an idiot for even thinking it (in the nicest possible way). It seemed as if they thought I'd be able to do some of the games, but that managing every single one would be a step too far. That left me a bit more fired up to go out and prove them wrong, but to an extent I could understand why they were a little sceptical.

The game was unremarkable, save for the fact that it went to a penalty shoot-out. After a disappointing Dons side had been held to a 1-1 draw by League Two Cheltenham, Robinson's side redeemed themselves by tucking away five superb spot-kicks to win the shoot-out 5-3 and book a place in the second round of the League Cup. What I will remember most about that afternoon was the superb support our travelling band of around 400 Dons fans gave our team. Radar, one of the regular away fans, was orchestrating most of the songs as usual, and towards the end of the game, he and others around him decided we should push the boat out.

"MK ARMY, MK ARMY, MK ARMY!"

The chant got louder and louder, and after a couple of minutes, something within us all decided to keep it going. It continued through the last ten minutes of the match, then the stoppage to reset for extra time, and then the entirety of both halves of extra time. We're normally pretty good as a set of fans for making noise away (definitely much better than we are at home), but even by our standards, that was pretty special.

I managed to get a lift back with my bike on the fans coach thanks to a kind offer by Motts Travel, and was met back at stadium:mk by Margaret, who had travelled back with Nicola. As became the normal routine, my kit went in the washing machine as soon as I got home and my bike was prepared for a cleaning and an oiling. I sat down later that evening and contemplated what I'd done. Having got the first ride out of the way, I decided it'd be best just to take things one ride at a time and try not to get overawed by the enormity of what I'd taken on. The last ride to Stevenage was well over eight months away, and in the short-term I had ten days to prepare for the first League trip of the season, a long haul down to the south coast for a Tuesday night fixture at Bournemouth. At 130 miles, it would be the longest ride I'd ever done in my life up to that point, but I had a whole day to do it. I was sure that I'd be all right.

CHAPTER 3: WHICH WAY TO DEAN COURT?

Alan Smith was right. Cheltenham was a pretty straightforward one to start with. Despite me being taken aback by the amount of climbing I had to do over the Cotswolds, it really wasn't that difficult in the grand scheme of things. Bournemouth was going to be something else altogether.

The Dons' winning start to the season had continued after Cheltenham, with a 2-0 victory at home against Oldham Athletic kicking off the new League season in fine style. This gave me an extra bit of motivation come 9:00am on the Tuesday morning after that game (August 21), as I set off from home on the long 130-mile road to Bournemouth.

While I had been planning the whole event, the question of where to start had arisen. After many long and tortuous debates with the dog, I finally decided that the most consistent start point would be stadium:mk. Annoyingly, it was ten miles in the wrong direction for Bournemouth. I set off with enthusiasm though, heading north on the A5 and arriving at the stadium reception. "Is Dennis around?" I enquired. Dennis Woolford had become my main point of contact at the Sports and Education Trust, but he was off-site at a local school in nearby Bletchley running the community sports programme that day. Getting back on my bike, with the slightly disappointing feeling that comes of not getting a little bit of a send-off, I thought I would go by the school.

When I arrived, I found out that Dennis had gone to

pick up one of our star first-team players, Stephen Gleeson. I hung around and waited, thinking of a potential photo opportunity. At about 10:30, the young Irishman turned up and the kids on the playscheme crowded around him for pictures. With a slight look of bemusement, Stephen cheerfully signed autographs and posed for photos, and eventually I got to nip in for a picture myself. I said to Stephen that I really appreciated his time to take a picture and we started talking about my project. I said I was just about to head off to Bournemouth. He looked surprised and took a moment to think about how far away it was from Milton Keynes. After his pause, he said: "So how are you going to get there – on the motorway?" Things are clearly different this side of the Irish Sea…

I headed off, the wind behind me and the sun shining, fully confident that I'd make it to Bournemouth's Dean Court ground in good time for the 7:45pm kick-off. Thanks to my past cycling experience, I more or less knew the first half of the route in my head. I kept a series of milestones in my mind heading south from Milton Keynes: through Aylesbury, Thame and down to Wallingford, crossing the River Thames at Pangbourne and carrying on to the A4 past Aldermaston. Given this was my first real test of endurance of the season, that first section had some significance for me as Pangbourne had been where I'd trained for the Devizes to Westminster Canoe Race all those years ago.

From there, however, things started to get a little hazy. It was a nice day, and having reached the approximate half-way mark, I stopped for lunch just after 1:00pm. So far, so good. But as I set off again, things started to get tough. I was still using my handwritten notes at this point, so I was on a wing and a prayer trying to remember the route I'd chosen through the Berkshire and Hampshire countryside to reach the south coast. I was travelling down a particular road, and I knew I had to turn left at some point. From what I remember, I was travelling west from

Aldermaston and needed to turn left to head south towards Andover. But I couldn't remember exactly which road I was supposed to turn onto.

Sure enough, I missed it. Out came a piece of paper that was sweaty and illegible from my handling it by this point, along with my phone so that I could try and decipher just where I'd gone wrong. Then I realised that I was in a location so remote that I couldn't get a good enough signal to load up the mapping app on my phone. Which meant I had to guess.

I was parked up at the side of what was a fairly narrow country lane, trying to work out what to do, when this strange woman came pootling along in her car. She stopped when she reached me, rolled down her window and just stared at me. After a few seconds she shouted: "I can't see you, you know!", after which I pointed out that I was well off the road and not a danger to any traffic. She decided against responding to this, instead staring at me in silence for about another minute before rolling up her window and pootling off down the road again.

I maintain to this day that that woman put a curse on me, because for the rest of the day it seemed that just nothing could go right. I set off again, resolving to stop and ask for directions from the first person I saw. After five bemusing miles, I saw a man stood at the roadside. "Is this the road to Andover?" I politely enquired. "Ay - no Eengleesh!" returned the undoubtedly foreign response.

I cracked on and eventually found a main road towards Andover, onto which I turned so I could regroup. Shortly after I had turned left, the entire contents of my saddle bag (the small bag hooked up underneath my saddle) spilled out onto the road. This included my puncture repair kit, spare tyres, various other tools and my snacks for extra energy. I was sure I hadn't left it undone earlier in the day, so the general bumps and movements of the bike must have gradually jiggled the zip open. Things were definitely not going right: I had no idea where I was, and now I had to pick half of the Halfords bike accessory range up off the A343.

If this had happened on a straight bit of road, then I would have had plenty of views of the traffic approaching and therefore could have gathered up my bits and bobs fairly easily. But as I was clearly having a bumbling afternoon that Mr Bean would have been proud of, it had happened on the inside of a blind bend. This reduced me to running sorties in and out of the road, dashing in, grabbing one thing and diving for the safety of the grass verge before regrouping for another go. After several repetitions of this bizarre exercise, I'd managed to recover everything – except for one Allen key. And yes, it was the one Allen key which fits just about every single tightenable hole on the entire bike. I spent 20 minutes on my hands and knees scuttling around a verge looking for it, thinking 'what the hell am I doing here?' before I eventually found it.

I then set off on my way again (with the saddle bag zip yanked up as tight as it would go, and then some), heading past Andover. After a brief scare in which I nearly went up the slip road onto the busy A303 dual carriageway, I plugged on south towards Stockbridge, but I'd realised that all my route-planning boobery had added a further ten miles to my journey. All I could do was forget that, put it behind me and crack on, as there was nothing I could do to get the distance back.

I reached Romsey, just north-west of Southampton, late in the afternoon. I was hungry, thirsty and equipped with a phone almost out of battery. I managed to beg the staff in the local Carphone Warehouse to charge my phone up while I went in search of grub, and got back on the bike with an extra push of effort as I was running out of time. It was 5:00pm by the time I remounted, and I practically time-trialled, Bradley Wiggins-style, past Lyndhurst and right through the New Forest. I briefly cycled with a chap who turned out onto the road in front of me. Turned out he was cycling down to Poole from Romsey. He was on his bike because he wanted to avoid being in the car at the same time as his wife and his mother-in-law. Although I struggled to keep up with him for more than about five miles, the benefit of riding with someone else really got me going. But I'd reached the stage where it seemed like the journey would never end. Lamp-post after lamp-post, white line after white line and (especially in the New Forest) tree after tree after sodding tree.

Once out of the forest, I found a road that remains to this day one of my favourite roads in Britain. Imagine a road with a smooth glass-like surface that gently bends downhill for about 10 miles. Bliss. I rode it at break-neck speed all the way down into Bournemouth, to find that the ground was nowhere in sight, and my handwritten notes were now beyond useless as they'd disintegrated through my sweaty, grubby hands. I wasn't lost. I just didn't know where to go.

As I pulled up at a set of traffic lights, a guy on a moped drew alongside. He told me to turn left at the next roundabout, which I did. After a mile downhill thereafter, on a road bereft of football supporters, I stopped and asked someone else for directions. My suspicions were correct. He'd sent me the wrong way. I was going to have to labour all the way back up said hill, much to my frustration. But eventually, after badgering half of Bournemouth for directions as if I was Anneka Rice on *Treasure Hunt*, I made it to Dean Court at 7:00pm, later than I'd intended but still in time for the match.

And that, at that point, was my greatest cycling achievement ever. In my euphoric state, it even knocked the Devizes to Westminster for six. John Samuel, Margaret and Nicola were there to meet me (although I was so late that a lot of the others waiting to meet me had lost interest and cleared off for a pint). But for the first time, more than three months after initially committing to the adventure, I felt like I'd actually achieved something. I felt as if I was well and truly up and running.

I had contacted Bournemouth to see if they could help me out with changing facilities, but sadly, they couldn't. They'd been a bit rude about it all, to be honest. However, a fan redeemed the club to me. She said I needed somewhere decent to change and the best place was a disabled toilet inside. Being the firm type, she strode up to the bouncer who was on the door and told him I was coming in to do the necessary. The poor guy wasn't given a choice and I managed to get a wash and change after all. To their credit, Bournemouth did later apologise for their lack of co-operation.

The game itself finished 1-1, with Alan Smith being given a harsh red card for a typically robust tackle early on. It wasn't an ideal result, but it was still certainly a good one away to an expensively-assembled team widely expected to challenge for promotion. Margaret and I had decided to stay in a local hotel overnight before travelling home the next day, and so after packing up the bike post-game and checking in, we headed down to the bar for a debrief and a few drinks. Time ran on and by 1:00am, I was absolutely ravenous. Bournemouth is hardly teeming with haute cuisine at 1:00am on a Wednesday, so a scabby kebab it had to be. Sitting there in the early hours, chomping on a dodgy doner, I felt strangely great, like a four-year-old showing off the Lego castle he'd just built to all his mates. The good feelings appeared to spread to the kebab, which tasted just about tolerable, which was amazing in the circumstances (bear in mind that I was tired and emotional at this point!).

It would be another month before I would have to attempt another ride of that length, and so armed with the confidence of what I knew I was definitely capable of, the next three trips passed off without any serious dramas. Just four days after Bournemouth (Saturday August 25), I faced another trip south and west to Swindon Town. The ride came in at 70 miles, so only marginally longer than

Cheltenham, and I knew the route there off by heart, so there was very little chance of enduring a repeat of my Bournemouth ordeal. The only happening of note en route to Swindon was riding through a tiny rural village while photos were being taken of a wedding party. With the photographer one side, the bride and groom on the other, and no time to stop, there's now a very unhappy couple somewhere in Wiltshire with a two-wheeled blur obscuring their wedding-day snaps. Erm, sorry about that...

Many football fans dread a trip to Swindon Town, for a variety of reasons. One is that it's not a particularly salubrious place to visit. Another is that the team's manager at the time of this fixture, Paolo di Canio, has always been a divisive figure in English football, to put it mildly. And the third is that many fans resent having to pay £25 (the most expensive away tickets at any League One team) to watch third-tier football from a corner of the ground, in a crummy antiquated stand still fitted with ramshackle wooden seats. But I, on the other hand, was very much looking forward to my afternoon at the County Ground, because Swindon had been the first team I'd visited to really embrace what I was doing.

Before each trip, I would always get in contact with the club I was preparing to visit, to see if they were will to help my cause in any way (as I've mentioned, I'd had little luck with Bournemouth). Over the course of the season, it was fascinating to notice which teams made an effort to help me out and/or donate, and which teams simply couldn't be bothered. If you thought the big teams were automatically more generous than the little teams, think again! Swindon, one of the better-backed teams in League One but certainly no Manchester United, bent over backwards to help me out, to the point that they probably would have allowed me to bend the club secretary over and use his buttocks as a bike rack if I'd so desired (I didn't).

After I got in touch with Swindon officials, I'd received

speedy replies from representatives of the club and the supporters trust to offer me changing facilities when I arrived and also to arrange a presentation for me in the bar. For the new season, Swindon had converted a room underneath the away section on the outside of the ground into an away supporters' bar, complete with pictures of the visiting team's players. The fact that we'd only had two League games previously made the effort of getting snaps of Dons players in their new kit an extra-nice touch.

When I arrived at Swindon, it was pouring with rain, but that didn't stop a little group of Swindon supporters turning out to meet me. I'd been on Radio Wiltshire that morning and they'd heard me, and were more than welcoming. Our little group had to be broken up for the late arrival of the MK Dons supporters coach, which had had to turn back because the team coach had forgotten to take a shirt for Daniel Powell to play in. I was then led away by the Swindon Town commercial director to my own private changing room (the reserve team changing room), complete with hot showers, soap and shampoo. "I could get used to this!" I thought.

As I came into the bar in my civvies, all the usual Dons away fan regulars were already in there, making the most of the new facilities that had been provided for them. There I was joined by Swindon's supporters trust chairman, commercial director and even the chairman himself, as they announced that they were donating £50 to my cause. It doesn't sound like a great deal, and in the great scheme of things, it wasn't. But the fact that a club like Swindon was willing to help out a charitable quest of another club, and not just any club, but the so-called 'franchise club', meant a great deal to me. Even if their fans aren't the most liked in the land, from this day forward I will always have a lot of time for Swindon Town, even though the Dons lost the game 1-0, captain Dean Lewington being sent off for violent conduct. The opposing set of fans thoroughly enjoyed that one, but some things never change…

Back at home the following week, results picked up, with an impressive 2-1 win over Championship table-toppers Blackburn Rovers in the second round of the League Cup followed by a 2-0 League win over Carlisle. The Tuesday after that (September 4), fate had handed me an extra trip for the first round of the Johnstone's Paint Trophy, but at least it was a short one – 22 miles north to Northampton Town.

I decided this was a great opportunity to try something special, and to put the emphasis onto speed rather than endurance. I saw no reason why I couldn't get there within an hour, and with a big crowd of visiting Dons fans expected, I reckoned that with a little bit of a head-start, I could attempt to beat the supporters' coaches there and try to raise a bit of awareness for what I was doing in the process. The coaches were due to leave at 5:15pm, so I set off from stadium:mk at 5:00 and quickly slipped the carbon-framed Giant into the biggest cog it's fitted with.

My friend Chris Reading came down to take some photos as I left, and as I headed onto the A5 trunk road, I got my head down and seriously started to mash the pedals. I had to travel up the A5 past Stony Stratford, onto the A508 through the village of Roade to junction 15 of the M1, and then around the Northampton ring-road system to Sixfields. I'd estimated that I could get to Roade before the coaches passed me. Any further than that before being passed would be a bonus.

As I came through Roade, I was powering along close to 30mph through the village, meaning the coaches weren't going to go any faster than me at that stage. As I went over a roundabout, I sensed a coach coming up behind me. It came past me as we came out of the 30mph zone, but as it did so, I realised that it wasn't one of our coaches. It was just 'a coach'.

Empowered, I picked the pace up a notch to the full maximum, hopeful that I might make it over the M1 and maybe even as far as Sixfields before I was caught. In an adrenalin-fuelled frenzy, I fired over junction 15 and carried on up the A45. I turned left onto the ring road and then had a heart-stopping moment as a car transporter came within inches of me as it overtook. I could almost feel its tyres graze my right leg as it came past, and the only reason I wasn't completely spooked by it was that it all happened in about two seconds. By the time it had sunk in what I'd narrowly averted, I was 400 yards up the road and just had to press on.

I dropped down a hill and as I approached a roundabout, the lights went green. Keeping the pace high, I flew across the roundabout and saw the coaches held up at the red lights to my left. I was still in front – just! I wasn't going to lose that close to Sixfields and I stood on the pedals, moving over into the right-hand lane so they couldn't overtake me. I swung into the Sixfields car park seconds before them, and just 52 minutes after leaving stadium:mk. I'd done it! OK, I needed a head-start, but I still think it was a great feat nonetheless.

It's strange that what was the shortest ride of them all had such an impact on the Dons fanbase and their attitudes towards me. A healthy away turnout of 1349 came to Northampton (unfortunately to watch us lose 1-0 and be eliminated from the JPT), many of whom had come on the coaches and had seen me attempt a ride first-hand for the first time. The trickle of donations that started to come in after that told me that I'd managed to get the project embedded into the backs of people's minds, and that would prove to be a great help to me as the season wore on.

The following Saturday (September 8), I took on a 77-mile ride to Walsall, just to the north-east of Birmingham. This would have been a nice easy ride on roads I pretty much knew, if I hadn't tried to ride through Coventry city centre on the way. I wasn't intending to do that to, but just one wrong turn and mis-remembered route note ruined the whole thing, and left me stranded in the middle of a plaza with seemingly no way out. I needed to head northwest to Corley (best known for the nearby service station on the M6), and asked a passing traffic warden for the best route. In the thickest Brummie accent you can imagine – it could have been Nigel Mansell if I had my eyes closed – he said: "I don't know, mate. I only know the way in an' the way out!"

Through luck more than judgement, I made it out and skirted around the east of Birmingham to Walsall. They were great as a club, the supporters trust chairman trying to get me out on the Bescot Stadium pitch for a half-time interview, although sadly that didn't materialise. Nonetheless, things were starting to pick up, and I had two whole weeks to rest and relax before the first proper long haul up to Lancashire, and our game at Bury.

The trip to Gigg Lane was the first of the rides that I'd had to divide into two days, and thanks to Sarah's hotel magic, I was able to ride a short first leg and stop at the Holiday Inn Express in Tamworth on the Friday night before completing the run to Bury on the Saturday (September 22). Tamworth is around 60 miles from Milton Keynes, which I thought would be short enough for me to cover on a Friday afternoon, meaning I wouldn't have to try and take a full day off work for it. Besides, I didn't much like the idea of trying to leave at about 2:00am on a Saturday morning and riding 150 miles in one go while stupidly tired.

Much like Northampton before it, I noticed another shift in attitudes from other Dons fans after I completed my ride into deepest Lancashire. I reckon it was then that the 'hardcore' support really started to think that I might actually follow up on my promise and complete the full set. After all, most of the other rides were significantly shorter than Bury, so I guess many people thought I'd done my hard bit (how wrong they were). And it wasn't just Dons fans noticing the difference, either: before I set off for Bury, *Look East* sent a film crew down to get some shots of me riding around stadium:mk and it seemed they were taking an interest in my story. Little did I realise at the time that I'd have to wait five months before the footage actually got used.

I thought the initial run up to Tamworth would be fairly simple as I left at 2:00pm on the Friday. But after barely half of that 60 miles, as I came through Daventry, I felt absolutely exhausted. It was as if I'd hit 'the wall' that I'd so often heard marathon runners talking about, when they feel absolutely fine and then suddenly feel completely devoid of energy. I pulled over and sat at the side of the road and thought: "I can't do this". This was the first time I hit a mental low, and as I carried on, I felt like I was just cycling for the sake of cycling. The weather didn't help, with rain gradually increasing in intensity and the wind picking up as I crawled my way north.

By the time I'd reached the hotel, I was struggling to pick myself up, especially as I'd had a major scare minutes beforehand. In the space of 30 seconds, I'd had to bunny-hop over a tree branch that fell into my path, had to cope with my glasses steaming up and then endured another near-miss, this time with a supermarket lorry. When I arrived at the hotel, I changed into my T-shirt and tracksuit bottoms – the only clothes I'd brought with me aside from my Dons shirt because I was expecting to be about ten degrees warmer than it actually was. I ended up eating my dinner in a restaurant in the Tamworth SnowDome (because it was the only place for food I could find) and went to bed thoroughly bloody miserable.

How things changed the following morning! The sun was shining, the roads were drier and in much better condition, and if anything I was able to enjoy the second leg of the trip, despite it being over 90 miles in itself. I romped through Staffordshire and into Cheshire, through Leek and Macclesfield and then into Manchester.

The previous season, I'd met a couple of guys from

Droylsden (an area of eastern Manchester) who had followed us through the FA Cup. They'd started the season by picking a team in the first qualifying round at random, going to all their games until they got beaten, and then following the team that beat them, and so on all the way to the final. They called this endeavour 'One Leg On The Cup'.

They had ended up with Nantwich Town in the latter stages of qualifying, and so wound up with us when we beat Nantwich in the first round. They came to watch us beat Barnet in round two, and both games in round three, where we lost to QPR in a replay. 1-Leg and Rhino (so-called as they are an amputee and a large man respectively) had become friends of mine, and so I met up with them at Droylsden FC, then in Conference North.

To say Droylsden has seen better days is a bit of an understatement but their hospitality was brilliant. I was taken onto the pitch and given a bit of a tour. They even gave me a scarf and told me to wear it for the rest of the journey to Bury; they said everyone would give me a wide berth because they'd think I was rock-hard.

After Droylsden, I took another detour to see the Manchester City ground, but I didn't get the same friendly reception, so after buying a badge, I carried on up to Bury.

A couple of miles short of Gigg Lane, I decided to put my Dons shirt on for a more appropriately-attired finish. Shortly after I started riding again, I got a shout from a passing car. I assumed it was going to be some Bury fans giving me some stick, but I saw that all the occupants were wearing Dons shirts like me. As I pulled into the car park, the driver got out and asked: "Did you just cycle here all the way from Milton Keynes?" I guess he hadn't heard about what I was doing beforehand. When I replied in the affirmative and waited for him to dismiss my reply as rubbish, he just beamed: "Fantastic!" I'd never met the guy before, but it felt like a breakthrough to me. People I didn't know were really taking notice, and it made all the hell I'd endured the previous day worthwhile. As did the steak pie (best in League One) and seeing the Dean Bowditch hat-trick that fired the Dons to a 4-1 win over the bottom-of-the-table Shakers.

Heading into October, things were looking up. I'd completed the first five League rides, the Dons were third in the table, and I was starting to receive some donations, which was the whole point of the exercise, after all. But with four away games in the month, I knew things weren't going to get any easier, but at least it started with a short Tuesday night trip to the Ricoh Arena in Coventry.

As a 50-mile ride that was only going to take me around three hours at full speed, I took the opportunity to bring some company with me for the ride. The Sport and Education Trust has its own fledgling cycling club, and they'd been in touch to say that some of them would like to come along with me. It was great to have them there on the day, although also a little frustrating in the sense that I was having to ride well short of my usual pace (and frequently stop) to allow them to keep up. These are people normally used to leisurely fun rides, and the certainly weren't prepared for the pace that a fit club cyclist with two months of long-distance rides under his belt could manage. Even though I took things easy by my standards, they all arrived in Coventry feeling like they'd been given an extremely thorough workout. For me, it was a walk in the park, which suggested just how far I'd come in the fitness stakes in such a short space of time.

Coventry had kindly offered Margaret and I seats in one of the hospitality boxes at the Ricoh for the evening, which we accepted. It was the first time I'd ever been in corporate seating at a football match. It was also the last time I will ever be in corporate seating at a football match. It wasn't just that I was in among the home crowd, preventing me from saying or shouting words of encouragement for the Dons as I normally would. It was the fact that I spent most of the game gazing jealously at the corner of the stadium where the 700 travelling Dons fans were singing their hearts out. They were my kind of people, and I just wanted to be among them. I felt detached from the game, the experience and dare I say it, from my own team. It's not an experience I ever want to repeat. I can't thank Coventry City enough for their hospitality, and I really don't want to sound ungrateful about the whole thing, but it just wasn't for me.

The whole experience also made me much more aware about involvement with other clubs in the future, especially my own. I was (and still am) a fan at heart, and this project was supposed to be about a fan helping out other fans, completely independent of the MK Dons organisation. The last thing I wanted was to be seen as a 'pet project' and have someone else jump on the bandwagon. I wanted to stand alone and make sure that all the publicity and the donations went through me to the beneficiaries of my efforts. It's for that reason that although I received several generous offers from MK Dons of corporate seats for home games throughout the season, I rejected every single one of them. Football is best enjoyed with your mates.

Some 12 days after Coventry, I faced what I knew was going to be one of the toughest rides I'd have to face all season – the two-day trip to Preston. It was going to be hard enough as it was, just because of the sheer distance of it, but to add insult to injury, Sky Sports had seen fit to select the game for live TV coverage. With it being on a weekend of World Cup qualifiers, there were no Premier League or Championship games that weekend, so League One enjoyed the limelight. The bad news for me was that to fit in with the Sky schedule, the game had been made a 1:15 kick-off on a Sunday lunchtime (October 14).

I'd planned to do a relatively short opening leg on the Saturday to Derby, before making a horribly early start on the Sunday to continue the ride into Lancashire. To minimise the amount of weight I'd have to lug around, I packed the bare minimum into the little bag that's strapped to my bike: a pair of flip-flops, some tracksuit bottoms, a jumper and a T-shirt, along with a little food. I gambled that that would be enough to cope with whatever the weather could throw at me.

I left the stadium on the Saturday lunchtime to rattle off the 70-mile ride to Derby fairly upbeat, thinking it was going to be easier than I'd perhaps suspected during my planning. I headed north through Kettering and Corby before skirting through Leicestershire, and I managed to get as far as Coalville before my mind just completely collapsed. All of a sudden, an extra ten or 15 miles ahead just felt like a bridge too far, and I just dropped onto a massive downer.

I stopped at a set of traffic lights, looked around and muttered to myself: "What the bloody hell am I doing here? I'm not good enough to do this. I'm not fit enough to do this. I'm sure as hell not enjoying it. This is just really hard work." I logged onto Twitter with my phone and tweeted something similar to this, but immediately as I did so, four or five people came straight back through with words of encouragement, which gave me a much-needed lift. "Come on, Adam," I said to myself. "Get yourself to Derby, and then you can sort yourself out. It's not too far. You'll be fine."

After arriving at the hotel, I made a beeline for the restaurant next door and did as much as I could to relax, both physically and mentally. I downed a couple of pints of coke, wolfed down a lasagne, and got down to an early (and very deep) night's sleep. The only think I could think of doing was to sleep through my misery, try and put it out of my mind, and hope that I'd wake up the next morning in a better frame of mind, much like I had on the way to Bury three weeks previously. I knew there would be dark days on this adventure when I started, but I don't think I was quite prepared for just how mentally taxing it would be at times.

STADIUM CHASE

It was around 3:30am that I awoke, two hours before my planned departure time for the 100-mile second leg. You know what it's like when you wake up and you know beyond doubt that you're not going to get back to sleep? That's exactly how I felt in that hotel room, staring up at the ceiling and letting my brain gradually reboot itself. With no hope of getting an extra hour's kip, I resolved to get up, check out, get on my bike and just get on with it. I didn't see much point in hanging around at that stage.

As I checked out at reception, the night porter offered to cook me some breakfast. After enquiring what I could get, he said that my best bet would be a panini. I asked for a bacon one, as well as a plain one with jam, and after having some cereal while I waited (I know it seems like a lot of food, but I had to take plenty of calories on board!). He looked at me tucking into my bowl of cornflakes with a decidedly quizzical look on his face.

"Do you want me to wrap some of this food up, or are you going to eat all that now?" he asked.

"No, I'm going to eat all this now," I replied, in slight bemusement as to why a bowl of cornflakes and two paninis was apparently a feast worthy of Henry VIII in this part of the world.

Two minutes later, he returned with what can only be described as the biggest pieces of bread I have ever seen, one of which was filled with so much bacon that it probably would have been easier to shove a whole pig inside the panini wholesale. And then came the other one that I'd ordered. "I can't eat all this!" I thought. And I didn't, but I scoffed as much as I could, put the rest in my bag and set off up the road towards Buxton and the Peak District at around 4:30am.

It was a cold, dark Sunday morning, but there was a pleasant peace on the roads and that tranquility calmed my mind (certainly when compared to how it was the previous afternoon). It certainly helped take the edge off the chill in the air. I had to do plenty of climbing after leaving Derby, and after that I was rewarded by a long, gradual downhill section which I was able to merrily bomb down... and down... and down.

By this time, I had decided that handwritten notes were useless and my friend from the bike club had offered me the use of his Garmin. This was a serious bit of kit, with mapping facilities that could show exactly where I was and how many miles I had done, all wrapped up in a neat little digital parcel that sat in the middle of my handlebars. This ride was the first time I had used it, however, and I couldn't decipher much of the information it was showing me.

Given my concerns about Garmin, it wasn't long before I started to get suspicious about how much I was dropping. And then I saw the sign ahead, informing me that I was heading towards Matlock. Bugger. I'd gone the wrong way. I'd completely misread/ignored the directions the Garmin had given me and I'd gone about six miles off course, and so it was after 5:30am as daylight was beginning to vanquish the darkness by the time I'd corrected my mistake and rode into Buxton.

Made famous by its spring and consequently its mineral water production, there's a good selection of steep hills in Buxton. As I was riding through the town, I encountered a runner, out for early-morning training and who, somewhat impressively given the fact that I was on a bike, was keeping roughly the same pace as me. I climbed a hill, caught him up and asked him: "Is this the way to Furness Vale?" He nodded and told me to keep going straight ahead. As we climbed further, I saw him stop ahead of me as he reached the summit of this hill, and it really started to hit home that something didn't seem right. "Either he's an amazing runner, or I'm not riding very quickly at all today," I thought.

When I reached the same summit, I stopped for some chocolate, and he cheerily said: "Furness Vale straight on, you'll be fine." I thanked him for the advice, bent over my bike to put my food wrappers back in my bag… and when I stood upright again a few seconds later, I looked around to find the runner had completely disappeared. I genuinely had absolutely no idea in which direction he'd gone, and I couldn't see him either way. It was a surreal moment which helped me eat up the next few miles as my mind tried to work out how he'd managed to pull off such a vanishing act.

From there it was largely downhill, through Furness Vale, out of the Peak District, down to Stockport and then into central Manchester, where the one-way system combined with some heavy fog did its level best to outfox me and throw me off course. Even with the Garmin, I still wasn't completely sure about my bearings. I chanced upon the central bus station, and so thought stopping to check a local map would be a good idea to deduce just how I would find the right road to travel north into rural Lancashire. I saw a group of four men while I was in there, who had a good laugh when I asked for the best way to ride to Bury from here (I'd taken a different route compared to the Bury game itself as I'd had to go to Derby to stop overnight rather than Tamworth). They seemed bemused that I was cycling from Manchester as far as Bury. The facts that I'd already ridden from Milton Keynes and would be going onto Preston probably would have made their heads explode, so I decided to wave them goodbye and get myself out of Manchester.

I quickly reached Bury, after which I skirted around the south of Blackburn and turned left to arrive in Preston from the east. I'd assumed that my climbing duties had finished for this trip after coming through the Peak District, but soon after Bury I was proved wrong. Very, very wrong. The last 20 to 30 miles just went up and up and up. I was absolutely staggered at how much and how steeply I was having to slog through what I thought would be no more than rolling northern countryside. It was a firm knock to my confidence, after I felt like I'd aced the

Peak District, and I could feel another psychological low coming on.

However, the views from the top of the ridges kept my spirits up and I knew that the eventual downhill ride into Darwen would be epic. I reached the top of a ridge, from which you could see for miles in pretty much any direction, but the short, sharp ups and downs along it were really starting to drain my energy. Eventually, the drop into the town came and I was laughing to myself as the road hit the valley floor and the signs said Preston was only 15 miles away. I took a right turn, expecting (optimistically, I'll admit) to see a flat, relaxing stretch. Instead I was greeted with a wall of road rolling further and further upward. I looked at it, sighed, and thought: "I just can't do this."

And with that, I dismounted. There was a low wall at the roadside, in front of a terraced house, on which I took a seat and took another look at the road, and firmly told it: "Look, I'll deal with you in a bit. Just not now, all right?" Then out came the secret weapon - the second giant panini the night porter in Derby had made for me earlier that morning, and which I'd crammed into my bag for an emergency such as this. After I'd made it disappear in about 20 seconds flat, a woman came out of the terraced house, took one look at me and asked: "Are you all right, love?" in that motherly, sympathetic way that only northerners can. I said I was fine and just needed a breather before carrying on to Preston, and she replied with: "Don't worry love, you'll be fine. You can use my wall for as long as you need."

After about half an hour, I felt like I was in a good enough mental state to continue up this hill. It was as I was struggling along that I learned a great amount about my mentality and how I should approach adverse situations such as this one in the future. I was trying to take my mind out of the situation and tried to imagine myself as another person looking on at me riding, as if I was a disinterested party watching me in the Tour de France on telly with no comprehension of any pain I was suffering. It sounds like a load of psycho-babble, I know, but it really did help me get over the top and enjoy the descent into Preston to finish the ride.

As if the ride to Deepdale wasn't enough, I had arranged to meet the MKDSA FC fans' team at their game against the Preston supporters' team. It meant riding past the football ground and carrying on for another four miles to the training ground. It was there that I met Stephen Cowell, a brilliant guy from Preston, who had arranged for me to use the changing rooms at the pitch where the game was played and get a shower, although I had to get changed back into my cycling gear for the return journey. Stephen came along and had also arranged for me to store my bike in the ground during the game. It was another example of how people are so willing to help out complete strangers for a good cause!

The professional football game that day was a tetchy 0-0 draw (not what the Sky cameras wanted, although the Dons were denied a clear penalty when Charlie MacDonald was fouled late on). At half-time I refuelled with the local delicacy, a butter pie (which I did not enjoy one bit) and at full-time I collapsed into the passenger seat of Margaret's car for the drive back home. I was fast asleep inside a minute – hardly surprising.

I turned a metaphorical corner that day, as far as the whole season was concerned. Preston had proved to be a very significant ride in the context of the whole project, and I realised as such at the time. And I knew that if I could face those lows and face that kind of distance and still come through it, then I could do the same for any of my rides for the rest of the season. Never has a 0-0 draw had such a galvanising effect on me.

CHAPTER 4: THE HEEL OF GOD

The nine days I spent back at home and at work after that ride up to Preston gave me a bit of a chance to reflect on what I'd done so far. I'd completed eight rides, two of them long-hauls, and the attention I was getting from my fellow Dons fans meant that more donations were starting to come in. I was also starting to feel much more upbeat about what lay ahead, with the large mileages I was putting in starting to have a real positive effect on my fitness: not that I was a slob to start with, you understand…

On the pitch, the Dons had made a solid start to the season, if not an absolutely perfect one. The inconsistent form of Robinson's side away from home was being bailed out by an excellent run of results at stadium:mk, where comfortable 1-0 and 2-0 wins were becoming the norm. This left the Dons firmly in the play-off places, and still in the hunt for automatic promotion, although we all knew there would be many twists and turns in the promotion race between then and the end of the season in late April.

October ended with another Tuesday-Saturday back-to-back pair of rides, to Crawley Town, League One's new boys located down the road from Gatwick Airport in West Sussex, and then to Scunthorpe United in North Lincolnshire. I was especially looking forward to the former, as the route south would allow me to travel through central London and take in a bit of sightseeing. It was certainly going to be a very different proposition to the likes of the Peak District and the rural roads I'd become used to over the first two months of the season.

And coming just a few months after London 2012, it gave me a chance to stop for a photo at Buckingham Palace, and to emulate my heroes by riding down the Mall, where the Olympic cycling road races had finished (sadly, without a gold medal for Mark Cavendish).

The weather was dreadful as I left Milton Keynes and headed south on the A5 towards Dunstable, but even that couldn't dent my excitement. I travelled through Bedfordshire and Hertfordshire, easily passing through Dunstable, St Albans and Edgware, but it was soon after I came through Edgware that the reality of cycling in London properly bit. I'd managed a good 18mph average speed up until that point, but as the traffic started to build up and the ride became a much more stop-start affair, that immediately dropped to a frustrating 12.

This continued all the way down to Hyde Park Corner, when I was given a fright when I saw an old suited man (I presume he was a civil servant – he certainly looked like one) ride a rented 'Boris Bike' straight out across six lanes of traffic. He had absolutely no regard for what any of the vehicles (mainly taxis) behind him were going to have to do as a result. It was obvious from where I was that he'd jumped a red light, something that sadly was not an unusual sight on my trip across the capital.

I naturally want to defend cycling and cyclists, but it's extremely hard for me to do so when you see some of the flagrant disregard cyclists have for road traffic laws, especially in London. I consider myself to be a responsible cyclist, wearing a helmet and safety gear, making sure my lights are fitted and working, and obeying the traffic laws. But everywhere I looked in London, there were people without helmets wearing dark clothing weaving in and out of traffic. It is absolute stupidity, and it's no wonder that motorists get so wound up when they have to put up with that kind of behaviour on a daily basis.

At the other end of that scale, I'd decided that the safest way for me to cross London on a busy Tuesday afternoon would be to 'make friends' with the traffic around me. This meant indicating wherever appropriate, not overtaking things that had already overtaken me, and so on. I knew that from Edgware on, the traffic around me would likely be the same cars, buses and vans, travelling together all the way down to Hyde Park Corner, and that I'd then hook up with a different set after that, heading south on the A23 to Croydon and beyond.

The plan worked excellently, and I was able to strike up a conversation while waiting at traffic lights with a van driver who was on his way to Crawley himself (the town rather than the match). I joked that with the heavy traffic, I'd probably get there before him (bizarrely, I probably did, given that I was able to ease away from him as I pedalled through the southern edges of London), but that friendship was of great help to me when I suffered a frightening near-miss.

A Mercedes had tried to pull out of a side road right into my path, and I had very little time and very few options to take avoiding action. All I could do was swerve into the middle of the road and hope that whatever was alongside me would be able to give me some room. Mercifully, it was that same van driver, who had seen the problem coming and had already moved over slightly to give me a little bit of breathing space. That van driver really saved my bacon – bet you've never heard that coming from a cyclist before!

By this point, my mood had soured slightly because the horrible, wet, cold, foggy weather had washed out any plans I had to do some meaningful sightseeing, and so the day had merely become a long, urban ride towards my destination. I managed to get through towards Crawley without too many problems, although finding the football club when I got into Crawley itself proved difficult. Crawley have enjoyed an irresistible rise through the ranks of non-league football, and indeed this was just their second season as a League side. It was therefore unsurprising that the town centre wasn't absolutely teeming with Crawley fans, but I thought at least some of them would know where the football ground actually was. I was forced to grab my phone and check Google Maps to confirm that my Garmin directions were correct.

I arrived pretty early and went around to the Redz Bar, the watering hole for both home and away fans that's situated outside the ground behind the home terrace. It was pretty deserted (the Dons supporters coaches hadn't arrived by this point), but I had a drink and a friendly chat with the bouncers before walking back around to see if the travelling MK Army had arrived. They still hadn't. But as I stood there wondering what to do with myself for the next couple of hours, a man came running across the car park towards me and excitedly asked: "Are you Adam?"

The man introduced himself as Ewan Dunlop, the commercial manager for Crawley Town. He seemed extremely keen to help me out, and quickly ushered me inside the ground for some snaps pitchside and in the dugout, during which I also got to meet a few of the Crawley players. He was also keen to tap me for tips about endurance sports, as he said he was a cross-country runner in his spare time.

After this, I returned to the Redz Bar for the cheapest pie and chips I've ever had at a football ground (I thoroughly recommend this if your team ever plays Crawley away!), and then took my place on the away terrace for one of the worst games I had to endure all season. It wasn't just that we lost 2-0 (the first time all season that we'd lost a League game by more than one goal), it was the fact that the view from the tiny terrace at one end of the pitch was dire, and that it was so foggy that you couldn't tell what was going on at the other end. While the Preston trip started badly and gradually got better, it seemed that Crawley was quite the opposite.

The next morning, I was greeted by an email in my inbox from Andrew Cullen, the Dons' commercial director, which started along the lines of: "I know you're going to Scunthorpe on Saturday, so I wonder if you could do us a favour…" He then went on to detail the arrangements for the Mascot Olympics that was taking place on the Friday at Doncaster Racecourse. I was intrigued by this and happy to help, so I arranged for Nicola to transport the costume of Donny (one of the two cows that are the Dons' mascots – she would race as the other one, Mooie), while I rearranged my cycling plans.

It meant that I actually left for a Saturday afternoon game at Scunthorpe on Thursday evening, cycling up as far as Oakham to stay at the house of a friend overnight, before leaving very early on the Friday morning as I had to be in Doncaster by 11:00am. As I rode north, I wasn't too worried about the physical impact of the one-furlong (200-metre) dash along racecourse turf as I had an extra day to play with, but I was worried about the reaction I'd get from the mascots of other clubs. After all, MK Dons still aren't exactly the most popular club in English football.

As it turned out, I had no reason to worry. The atmosphere between the various mascots assembled was fantastic, and I found that while some of them were the 'proper' matchday mascot-wearing staff, others were volunteers wearing the costume for the day, just like me. Even the mascots from clubs we've had little rivalries with, such as Peterborough United, were warm and welcoming.

I'd arrived sweaty and tired, due to a heavy headwind all the way up from Oakham, and as I gathered my thoughts I discussed our race strategy with Nicola. We agreed that for maximum attention and exposure that we should either come first or last, and that if we weren't in contention to win, then we should fail as spectacularly as possible. Myself and the rest of the mascots with comedy feet were given a ten-metre head start over those who were just wearing trainers. The starter held us for what seemed an age and then, suddenly… GO!

My hopes of victory were extinguished inside five

seconds as the trainer-shod characters came speeding past. At this point, Nicola and I resolved to slow down a bit, ensuring that we crossed the line last of all and did a comedy belly-flop as we came past the finishing post. Then all hell broke loose, as the Bradford City Gent played along and tried to give me CPR, but the rest of the field saw it as a chance for a bundle and I quickly ended up buried underneath half a Football League of mascots! The chaos continued when we were all treated to a couple of corporate boxes, replete with some lunch and two very well-stocked fridges with a wide range of beverages, some of which were alcoholic. I'd had a bottle of beer and saw that things were starting to get a little carried away and remembered that I still had 20 miles to ride over the Scunthorpe, so I snaffled a couple of cans for later and sat and watched the racing before heading out to complete the ride alongside the Humber Estuary.

The first ten miles out of Doncaster were fine, but the last ten to Scunthorpe were extremely tedious. The north Lincolnshire landscape is flat as a pancake, largely featureless and very exposed to strong winds – all the things you don't want as a cyclist (bar Alps and rogue Mercedes, obviously). It was possibly the dullest bit of riding I've ever had to endure. Nonetheless, I eventually arrived at Scunthorpe's ground, Glanford Park, and duly got a few pictures taken as I completed my tenth ride of the season. Then I decided to decamp to my hotel for the night, the Berkeley, about 500 metres down the road towards the town centre.

I had some feelings of trepidation about this hotel, because it was £30 for the night and from what information I could gather on the internet, a pint of beer was about £1.60. I wondered what the hell I'd let myself in for. I remembered Dan describing to me this pub he'd been to in Scunthorpe before that sold cheap beer and was, in his words, 'bloody mega', but I'd assumed it was in town. I didn't realise it was this place! I'd suspected it was going to be some dive, but the Berkeley is a hotel that happens to have a Samuel Smith's pub on the ground floor (Samuel Smith's being a brewery that owns a large chain of pubs but that only sells its own products, hence the almost criminally low prices). It was an excellent way to end the evening.

Saturday started badly when I accidentally locked Nicola's keys in her car and we had to call the AA out to the Berkeley car park, but once that was sorted, we revelled in another big away win. The Dons claimed a 3-0 victory against a Scunthorpe team that really was one of the worst I'd ever seen us play against. Everything about their play was disjointed and disconnected, and their goalkeeper Sam Slocombe made a string of embarrassing foul-ups (to be fair to Sam, he got his revenge with a superb display when Scunthorpe beat us 1-0 at our place just before the end of the season). Only 160-odd Dons fans had made the trip north, many deciding a fourth away game in a month was too much for their bank accounts to bear, but those that did come up north had an absolute whale of a time. I know I certainly did over the three days of that trip.

Heading into November, and completing a run of three away games in 11 days, the next trip took me 50 miles east of Milton Keynes to Cambridge. We weren't playing the biggest team in the famed university city, Cambridge United, but tiny Southern Premier League team Cambridge City, four divisions below the Dons, against whom we'd been drawn away in the first round of the FA Cup. ESPN had sensed the chance of a giant-killing and had chosen to broadcast the game live, hence it being moved forward to the Friday night. The game had an extra bit of significance for me because it was the trip on which I passed the 1000-mile mark for the season. Cycling 1000 miles had been my original goal for the season, and so it gave me a great deal of satisfaction to reach that target within three months of the season beginning.

The ride itself was fairly straightforward (although I did have to ring some of our fans on the supporters coaches to advise them on how to get around the traffic jam they were stuck in on the A428). The only problem was finding Cambridge City's miniscule ground, Milton Road. Despite the fact that it was located very close to the city centre, none of the people I asked had any clue, despite the fact that my Garmin was telling me I'd arrived. Eventually, about the tenth person I stopped informed me that I was about 20 metres away from the main entrance, with the ground tucked away down a tiny side road. I know City are planning to move to a new ground in the near future – I hope it's easier to find than the old one.

I met Cambridge City's media man when I arrived at the ground, who ushered both me and my bike through to pitchside, where ESPN were recording various interviews with fans of both sides for its pre-game build-up. The producers clocked me and my bike and instantly knew there was something worth reporting on with me. They asked me to ride through the gates into the car park to get a shot of me 'arriving', a request I was happy to comply with. But after I'd done this, the cameraman said: "Ah, I didn't quite get that right. Can you do that again?" I was happy to get the exposure, so I didn't mind. But as I prepared to come through the gates one more time, a man on a town bike came rolling past me and up to the stadium, and the ESPN camera followed him in. So although I did get my bit of TV publicity, the action shot they used isn't me!

The atmosphere in the club bar prior to that game was wonderful. The whole thing was clearly a huge occasion for City: the extra gate receipts and TV money made an enormous difference for a club of that size: City normally played in front of a couple of hundred people for their league games, but this was practically a sell-out (although still only a crowd of 1800 as Milton Road was so tiny). They really had pulled out all the stops to make both MK

Dons and ESPN feel welcome: the City chairman bought me a pint as a 'well done' gesture, shortly before he was interviewed for TV himself. It was as I was enjoying that pint that I clapped eyes on a Dons legend wearing a bizarre three-piece tweed suit: Mad Dog was here!

Martin Allen (often referred to as Mad Dog) had managed the Dons for a year and had got us into the League Two play-offs in 2007 before he left for Leicester City, and he'd come to Cambridge to work as a pundit for ESPN. I approached him and asked for a photo, and the man he was with held my phone to take the picture. This man, who I didn't recognise as anyone famous, had a wry smile on his face as he took it, as did Martin, but I had no idea why. It was only later when I was talking to another Dons fan that I was asked why I had gone up to a lower-league manager to get a photo and asked Chris Waddle to take it for me!

By the time I'd done all this and had a short live interview with ESPN pitchside, I had just enough time before kick-off to cram myself into a toilet cubicle and get changed. I was lucky to be able to reach it; with TV people and so on, the tunnel area was covered in minders and security, but I'd been there so long and been in and out doing stuff that they all knew me and didn't mind. I got changed and came out of the toilets just before kick-off... to find myself in the middle of both teams lining up in the tunnel. I'd never been in this situation at any football match before, and it gave me a bit of an extra buzz.

I scurried round to the patch of tarmac where the Dons fans had been put (it wasn't even a terrace), and watched us be held 0-0 by a dogged, determined City team. Both Gleeson and Luke Chadwick hit the woodwork, and City's goalkeeper Zac Barrett pulled off some outstanding saves. It was the best result for City, who would now get even more cash by coming over to stadium:mk for a replay, while I was very confident that we'd be able to sweep them aside at home, where we were so strong.

Two days after that original game in Cambridge, however, the story of my season shifted dramatically. I was sat at home watching the draw for the FA Cup second round, waiting to see who we would have to play after (presumably) beating Cambridge City in the replay. The draw went on, and on, and still we hadn't come out. Then there were only a few balls left, and my eye was drawn to the name of one particular team on the graphic of the remaining teams still in the pot.

Then it happened.

"Cambridge City or Milton Keynes Dons... will play... York City or AFC Wimbledon."

At that point, both teams still had replays to get through, so the first meeting between the team that used to be Wimbledon FC, and the team founded by fans that used to support Wimbledon FC, was not yet a certainty. But sure enough, just over a week later, AFC got past York in extra-time in their replay, and we thrashed Cambridge City 6-1. It was on. And, predictably, it was soon confirmed that the match would be shown live on ITV. Being secretary of the MKDSA, this meant my cycling pretty much took a back seat for a couple of weeks as requests for media interviews and the like began to soak up a huge amount of my time. But I still had to do the rides as well, and I had a tough Friday-Tuesday double-header to Tranmere Rovers and Shrewsbury Town to navigate before the 'grudge match' came along.

The ride to Tranmere Rovers, in Birkenhead on the Wirral peninsula, was 149 miles. If the game been run to the normal schedule on a Saturday afternoon, I would have split the journey over two days. However, with us still at the sharp end of the table and Tranmere flying high at the very top, the Sky Sports telly gods interfered yet again and shifted us to a Friday night (November 16). Whilst all my friends were bemoaning this new situation, I was jumping up and down with glee! If I started early, I could cram the ride into a single (admittedly gruelling) day.

I set off at about 8:00am on the Friday and much of the route to start with was similar to that for Bury: up to Coventry and skirt around the east of Birmingham. I had aimed to stop for lunch at Rugeley, around the halfway point, but well before that I began to feel really queasy, to the point that I thought I might even have to pull over at the side of the road to be sick. It was as much as I could do to keep a cup of coffee down at my planned stop, but within a few miles, the beverage had made me feel better, but now I felt very hungry.

I started to look for a café or bakery where I could get something to eat, without success. I ended up on a mixture of very heavy dual carriageways and had no choice but to pull off onto a quiet country road on my way up to Nantwich, west of Crewe. Village after village passed by and my expectation of finding a café started to diminish. I was beginning to think I might have to settle for a chocolate bar from a petrol station somewhere. Finally, I saw a sign through a farm gate to a craft shop. With no expectation of anything other than a very expensive, chintzy tearoom, I made my way around the back of the farm to some refurbished stables.

Inside, all my dreams came true. I was cold, tired, hungry, and the site of a dozen pies lined up on the counter was the most heart-warming sight I could have hoped for. I immediately ordered a coffee and a slice of the most gorgeous-looking cherry tart I'd ever clapped my eyes on. Then, the kind lady behind the counter said the loveliest words I heard all season: "Would you like cream or custard with that?" If it had been socially acceptable to do so, I would have climbed over the counter and given the woman a big hug there and then. As I opted for the custard, I then spotted the deal of the day: a pork pie platter. Given my love of that particular savoury delicacy, that was immediately added to my order.

Half an hour later, I emerged from the cafe feeling like Popeye after he's just necked a can of spinach. Imagine me with bulging muscles, skipping back on to my bike and tearing off up the road at 1000mph, with the *Popeye* theme playing in the background, and you have a rough idea of how good I felt. And having been filled to the brim with my favourite foods, I absolutely battered the last 30 miles up to Tranmere's ground, Prenton Park. I practically time-trialled all the way up there, trying to keep my average speed up as high as I could. I felt magic when I arrived, despite misreading the road signs just outside Chester and almost ending up on the M53.

The only downer of the evening was trying to get changed. Despite the driver of the team bus again offering me the coach to get changed in, I decided to accept the Tranmere supporters club's offer of their toilet area as a goodwill gesture. I went in there to find the floor was largely covered in urine... which wouldn't have been a problem if it wasn't for the fact that Margaret had forgotten my shoes. I found the driest corner of floor I could find, and tried to wriggle in and out of my kit like Superman in a phonebox.

As I did so, a few Tranmere fans came in and out to use the facilities (don't worry, I didn't expose myself). Most were kind, but one apparently plastered local just seemed very angry with me for some reason. He obviously thought my riding a bike all the way there was a waste of time and energy, and cried: "What the hell have you done that for?! You're just gonna get beat!" Despite him repeating himself a dozen times, I did my best to politely ignore him. Funnily enough, later that evening, when the Dons pinched a superb 1-0 away win thanks to an 88th-minute Gleeson goal that took forever to trickle over the line. I thought: "Fan in the toilet, that one's for you!" Top-of-the-table Tranmere had over 10,000 fans in that night after making all tickets £5, and that attendance figure rapidly diminished after the goal went in. It was, without doubt, a sweet victory for me.

On the way home, I reflected on the ride I'd

completed, and I quickly realised that the fantastic last section I'd ridden wasn't just down to my being plied by treats at that cafe. A lot of it was to do with riding at night. It was getting dark by the time I'd left the cafe, with the clocks having gone back a couple of weeks previously, and I've always found myself going a little faster at night than during the day. I think this is because there's less for you to look around at in the dark, and it really focuses the mind and makes you concentrate on what you're doing on the bike.

Four days later, I got to put that theory to the test again when I had to ride to Shrewsbury for a Tuesday night game, my last ride before the AFC Wimbledon game at the beginning of December. I skirted around the south and west of Birmingham this time, and somehow managed to trump the cafe I'd found en route to Tranmere. At the halfway mark, I found myself at Henley-in-Arden. I pulled into the first cafe I found, which miraculously turned out to be a old cycling café. Cycling has its own culture and cafés play a big part in that. It probably goes back to the post-war period and the popularity of cyclo-tourism. Anyway, this one had lots of pictures of cyclists on the wall from that period.

Oddly, it transpired that this was primarily an ice-cream parlour. Bearing in mind the time of the year and that it was located nowhere near the seaside, I was slightly puzzled. All I could think was: "Who on earth is going to buy ice cream in a town in Warwickshire on a freezing Tuesday lunchtime in November?!" Then I was made to think differently when I clocked the size of the queue, which was practically snaking back to the front door. I guessed it must be some local 'cult' eatery. I decided against an ice-cream (I still thought it was an odd choice for November), and chose a bacon roll instead. The staff were really kind and even made a donation to my fund, and after a fine stop, I headed back off on the road to Shropshire.

I travelled west, away from Birmingham, with the intention of reaching Shrewsbury via Ironbridge, and it was around Ironbridge that the Garmin let me down for once. For some reason, it directed me down a farm track, and then onto a forest bridleway, on which I had to persevere for about three miles before returning to a more civilised highway. By the time I did so, my £3000 carbonfibre-framed bike was caked in what looked like about six tons of God-knows-what. To say I was miffed for the last 10-15 miles that followed to Shrewsbury was an understatement.

Martin, Shrewsbury Town's commercial manager, was a great help when I arrived, and sorted me out a shower in the changing rooms of the Powerleague five-a-side centre that sits right behind the away end. On top of that, he sorted Nicola, who had driven up, with a parking space literally right next to the away turnstiles, which was ideal for a speedy post-game escape. I also met up with the head of Shrewsbury's supporters trust, Adrian Plimmer. He was a really friendly guy and the chat inevitably turned to the AFC Wimbledon game. I've found over the years that some clubs have a much bigger problem with the existence of MK Dons than others, and Shrewsbury has always been one of those 'hardline' clubs. Adrian was pretty open about his views and we had a lively, but constructive talk. And as should always be the case, we parted friends and still stay in touch via the medium of Facebook!

During the game, the Shrewsbury Town fans, who situate themselves to the immediate right of the away end, gave us travelling Dons fans plenty of AFC-related stick, especially when the Shrews turned a 1-0 deficit into a 2-1 lead. At half-time, I was invited down onto the pitch to be interviewed by the pitchside presenter. Slightly nervous given the banter on the terrace, it was great that I could speak proudly about my recent 1000-mile achievement. The enthusiastic clap from the home fans that followed was really appreciated.

The game became really tight in the second half and despite what seemed our greatest efforts to turn a victory into a loss, a Dean Bowditch volley in the second minute of stoppage time silenced their fans and allowed a lacklustre Dons side to escape with a point.

That back-to-back run to Tranmere and Shrewsbury respectively didn't cause me any significant problems health or fitness-wise, even though they collectively accounted for over 250 miles of cycling. It hadn't even occurred to me that I might get any injuries or punctures, and it dawned on me that I'd been pretty lucky to avoid either over nearly 1300 miles of action up to this point. Then again, the distances were allowing me to reach a level of fitness I hadn't enjoyed for years, and it was certainly making things easier.

After Shrewsbury, I had a gap of two and a half weeks until my next away trip, and after watching the Dons claim a crushing 5-1 home win against Colchester United, the build-up to the AFC Wimbledon game the following weekend began in earnest. As MKDSA secretary, barely a day went by without me receiving a request for an interview, and our chairman, John Brockwell, was practically snowed under. The job we had to do was just as important as my cycling fundraising – we had to stick up for the fans of our club and put our side of the story across.

Probably the most important interview I gave was a week beforehand on BBC Radio 5 Live (not the last time I'd be on 5 Live during the season, but more of that later). Not only would I be on with Simon Wheeler, chair of the Wimbledon Independent Supporters Association (WISA), but the presenter was also a Wimbledon fan. I had six hours' notice of this happening, so I spent the entirety of that time doing as much preparation as I could for the 15-minute interview: coming up with questions I might be asked, writing down responses, and also reading up and re-reading up on the history of Wimbledon's move to Milton

Keynes to make sure I had my facts completely in order. Not only did the interview go very well, according to the people who listened and said I'd held my own, but I manage to wedge in a mention of my cycling right at the very end.

That wasn't the end of my dealings with the Beeb that week. We'd been invited to send someone to appear on the red sofa of *Breakfast* on the morning of the game (Sunday December 2). Due to the unique way the BBC is funded, that sofa now resides in Salford, Greater Manchester rather than in easy-to-get-to Shepherd's Bush. The producers insisted that whoever came up to Salford to do the interview at around 9:00 would be able to get back to Milton Keynes for the game itself, which kicked off at 12:30, but I just didn't have the confidence that I'd definitely get back in time.

Because of this, the interview, which would have taken place alongside a WISA representative, fell through. So imagine my surprise when, at the time I would have gone on, an AFC fan was interviewed from their ground in Kingston, with a BBC transmission unit having been dispatched to them. We were never offered this, which I thought was unfair in the extreme. Aside from that, I found a lot of the media circus that surrounded the game very fair and even-handed, and there was plenty of objective analysis of everything that went on across most (although not all) of the national newspapers. From an MKDSA standpoint, that was a mission accomplished, and the best we could have hoped for.

Amid everything, it was hard to remember that there was actually a football match surrounding all of this. stadium:mk (well, the bit with seats in it as the top tier still wasn't finished) was packed in the home sections, while the AFC Wimbledon supporters brought just over 3000 fans to MK, despite widespread talk of a boycott leading up to the match. It was a tight game, with AFC looking solid and organised in defence, and MK Dons looking scrappy and struggling to convert chances. Then, in first-half stoppage time, the ball rolled towards an open Gleeson, about 35 yards out. And as soon as he hit it, you knew it was going in. Inch-perfect, the ball escaped the grasp of Neil Sullivan (a former 'keeper for the original Wimbledon) and slammed into the top-right corner of the net in front of the AFC fans. Three sides of stadium:mk erupted.

After half-time, it was clear that we needed a second goal to kill the game off, but AFC returned fresh and determined. A cross came in on the hour mark with AFC's star striker Jack Midson met with a perfectly timed diving header to make it 1-1. It was one of very few strong attacks of the match from AFC, but it worked. And so the nerves set in, both for me and for the team (once the AFC fans had been cleared off the pitch and the match could restart). I genuinely couldn't see where we were going to score a winner from.

And then, with about 20 minutes to go, the reality dawned on me. A replay. In Kingston. I was going to have to ride down there.

For the remainder of the game, I could think of nothing else. Margaret was sat beside me and I asked her what she thought I should do. She was fairly unequivocal about it.

"No. You shouldn't go. It isn't worth it."

Initially, I concurred, but it took about three minutes for my head to turn that around completely.

"You know what, I'll go," I told Margaret. "I'm going to be the bigger person about this. This isn't about me and football politics, this is about me and fundraising for kids who want to learn and who want to play football. I've made a promise and I've got to stick to that."

At ten minutes to go, and with the score still 1-1, I began to think of the logistics of riding to AFC Wimbledon away. The actual ride to the Kingsmeadow ground in Kingston, south-west London, wouldn't be a problem. I was more concerned about avoiding any confrontations with AFC fans. As I'd already seen at this game, emotions would inevitably be running high. I mentally discussed things with myself.

"Do I get there early, Adam?"

"No, that wouldn't work, Adam. Where would you go when you get there?"

"OK, fair point, Adam. Well, I'll ride in at the same time as the supporters' coaches, then. Safety in numbers."

"So you're going to need to find some sort of police escort, then? And how are you going to meet up with the coaches on the way in?"

"Yeah, that'd be difficult. All right, I'll go down the day before then."

"Now you're talking. Cycle down there the day before, get some pictures while it's quiet, and then you can go to the game on the coach with everybody else. That sounds like a good compromise to me."

As I reached this compromise, the game was a minute into stoppage time. Dean Bowditch had floated in a Dons corner, which had landed in the AFC penalty area and resulted in a desperate goalmouth bundle. The ball broke loose outside the box, left of centre, where teenager Zeli Ismail, on loan from Wolves, drilled it back in to the melee. The ball came towards our right-back, Jon Otsemobor, who was ambling around the penalty spot with his back to goal. With what looked like total nonchalance, he stuck out his right foot, and without looking at where he was aiming, the ball bounced off the side of his heel and looped towards goal. It was high. It looked like it was going just over the bar. Then it started to dip. Then you could tell that Sullivan's outstretched hand wasn't going to reach it. It dropped down behind him and nestled in the bottom-right corner of the net.

I jumped out of my seat and screamed. So did Margaret. So did the other 13,000-odd people in the home section of the stadium. Some Dons fans were on the pitch.

They thought it was all over. It wasn't then, but it might as well have been. The AFC players looked deflated and dejected as every single Dons player ran to the home touchline and swamped Karl Robinson. The last few minutes of stoppage time passed without major concern, the full-time whistle went, and the monkey was well and truly off our backs. And I wasn't going to have to ride down there for a replay.

What happened that day has little to do with my cycling adventure, which is what this book is all about. But I make no apology for including it. Because as much as my story continues (especially as the FA Cup third-round draw held a few minutes later handed me a trip to Sheffield Wednesday), Sunday December 2 2012 well and truly closed the book on the first chapter of the history of MK Dons.

We had been given some closure: we'd been made to face our dark past square in the face, and came through it with dignity. I think we earned the respect of some other parts of the football community too. If we hadn't, then the continued sniping from AFC Wimbledon and others through the media would have carried on after the game. But there was nothing. I tuned into 5 Live and listened to *606* after the game. The presenters, Mark Chapman and Robbie Savage, both came to the same conclusion about AFC Wimbledon, along the lines of: 'You've got your own club now, what's happened has happened, move on.'

That game allowed everything that had happened to be given its airing in the media, and now that the two teams have played each other, it's no longer an issue. As I write this piece, some seven months after that game, I haven't heard a peep from AFC Wimbledon or WISA in public criticism against us since Jon Otsemobor scored *that* goal. And I don't expect that to change any time soon.

CHAPTER 5: RIDING TO NOTHING

After beating AFC Wimbledon, everything returned to normal and I was able to properly focus on my cycling again. We had just two more away games before Christmas, after which we had another match on the road on January 1, and so it seemed that the festive period would be relatively kind to me.

Six days after Jon Otsemobor's moment, quickly christened 'The Heel of God' by Dons fans (Dan had even gone to the lengths of making special T-shirts to commemorate the event), I faced a short ride to Brentford, not too far from the place I was so dreading riding to for the FA Cup replay that never happened. For this trip to west London, I genuinely thought I could beat the supporters' coaches. While I headed through urban London, the coaches would have to take a more circuitous route, around the M25 then passing Heathrow Airport on the M4 and reaching Brentford that way.

A couple of people doubted me, insisting that the lower average speeds through London that I'd experienced en route to Crawley would strike again, and that a 45-mile ride was too much for me to 'beat the buses'. Sadly, they were right. The coaches beat me by a full 40 minutes, and so despite riding from Milton Keynes to Brentford in about two hours (still no mean feat, on reflection), I was feeling pretty hacked off with myself. I didn't even have time for a drink when I got there, and I had to get changed on the team coach as Brentford just didn't have any space for me to do so inside Griffin Park. The Dons lost as well, a 2-1 lead being turned into a 3-2 defeat by a Brentford team that looked good for promotion, and so it was a miserable day all round for me.

I then had a two-week break to pick myself up before my last ride of 2012, up to Doncaster Rovers. By the time December 22 rolled around and I made my journey to South Yorkshire, the Brentford ride had been my only away trip in a month. I used the spare time to get back into my usual routine of training rides, something which had been disrupted with all the midweek games in autumn, so I set off for Doncaster feeling fresh and prepared. What's more, I'd already ridden the entire route to Doncaster as I'd travelled there (and run down a racecourse dressed as a cow) en route to Scunthorpe, so I already knew exactly what lay in wait.

Unfortunately, as you've probably come to realise by this stage, it's never that simple for me. The weather the day before the game was horrendous, not just in Milton Keynes or Doncaster, but pretty much across the whole country. The temperature wasn't far above freezing and there was torrential rain, which led to heavy flooding all around England and beyond. A number of lower-league games had been called off due to waterlogged pitches, but it seemed as though the Keepmoat Stadium had escaped the worst, and as I prepared to leave at 5:00am on the last Saturday before Christmas, the game was still very much on.

The only thing that saved me that day was the tailwind. Or rather, to describe it more accurately, the tail-gale. A strong wind blew me north all the way from start to finish, and made the biblical showers I had to deal with marginally more palatable. I was able to average almost 19mph along much of the route, an impressive return by my standards for a 120-mile ride where pacing myself was important.

Margaret was convinced that the game wouldn't be on, and tried to talk me out of hitting the road in that weather. However, my belief in the new facilities at the Keepmoat made me think that the risk was worth taking. Plus, I would look a bit pathetic if the rain stopped. I went straight up the A5, past Pink Punters, the LGBT club in Bletchley. At 5:00am, it was still going strong (Dan, ever the nightlife aficionado, later informed me that it doesn't normally close until 6:00am on a Friday night). Not for the first time, I felt a bit outside the norm of society and carried on north. I didn't see the point of spending extra time in the rain by fiddling about at stadium:mk in the dark, so I carried straight on past it. The wind was pushing me along and although it was raining, I was thoroughly enjoying myself. At around 7:00am, I was passing through Kettering when my phone rang. It was Margaret.

"Look," she protested. "The weather's not getting any better. It's just as bad in Doncaster. I can't see how this game could possibly be on. I really think you should turn back."

I was already 40 miles in by this point, and I was mindful of the fact that turning back and heading for home would be even greater torture because that tailwind would suddenly become a headwind. So strong was this wind that I felt it would have been just as easy (and I use the word 'easy' in its loosest sense) to complete the 80 remaining miles to Doncaster than ride the 40 back home. So, armed with my credit card, which I decided to bring with me so that I could get a train home if I got stuck, I carried on regardless.

The route remained familiar, up to Oakham and

beyond. I arrived at Oakham at about 8:00am and as there were no cafés open, I was forced to find shelter and eat my slightly damp peanut butter sandwiches. The only place that could afford any shelter was a ditch behind a hedgerow. It was a bleak existence. The road continued through the Vale of Belvoir and soon enough, I was in Newark. The town is, of course, situated on the banks of the River Trent, and all the rain that had fallen over the previous hours and days had swelled the river to enormous levels. The road I took through Newark runs along the riverbank, so I was able to see first-hand the raging torrent of water that was rushing downstream.

I reached a big roundabout near the centre of town and found a sign informing me that the road I needed to take was closed. I didn't need the delay of trying to find an alternative route, so I thought: "Bugger this, I'll go down here anyway." A couple of hundred yards down the road, I saw no reason why it should be closed and thought that I'd be fine and be able to merrily carry on my way. Then I came around a corner and saw exactly why it was closed. The entire road was completely flooded.

The Trent had burst its banks, and the road and fields immediately next to it had been swamped. The road dipped down, therefore making the bottom of that dip particularly submerged, and on the other side, perhaps 200 metres away, I could see the road rising up beyond the surface and carrying on. To my left, there was a cycle path raised around six inches above the road level. I didn't think the water level on the road was more than 30-40cm deep, and that the water covering the cycle path would therefore be even shallower, and probably no worse than riding through a puddle. Given the choice of riding through this water, or turning back and having to take a very long way round that I wasn't definitively sure of, I opted to go for it.

To start with, everything seemed fine. Then the pavement dropped down to what I presume was the road level. I say 'presume', because the water was so brown and muddy that I couldn't see below it. That gave me a bit of a fright as the water level came up and over the contact patch of my tyres, but still I soldiered on. Then I hit a bump and my rear light fell off, forcing me to go scavenging in the muddy water with my hands to find it. Miraculously, as I plunged my hands into the liquid unknown for the first time, I found it straight away, and perhaps more miraculously, it still worked as I reattached it to my bike and escaped the flood zone.

I felt like a big kid going on an adventure by careering my bike through the newly-created ford, a feeling exacerbated when I spoke to my mum the following day and told her about it.

"You should never ride through flooded water," she scolded. "You never know what's going to be in there. What if the flood water had blown a manhole cover off, and you'd ridden into the hole?"

She was right. On reflection, it was a fantastically stupid thing to do. If she'd said those words to me before I'd reached Newark, I probably would have turned back and found another way around. And I'd certainly do that now if I'm ever faced with a similar situation in the future. But at that time and at that moment, I'd got away with it, and kept on mashing the pedals in the general direction of Doncaster.

Eventually, I reached the McDonald's at Markham Moor on the A1, around 20 miles south of Doncaster: a fast-food eatery that would become a personal sanctuary on all my rides to that part of the country over the course of the season. It was pouring with rain by this point, and out of the windows in every direction, there were just buckets of rain falling, to the extent that you simply couldn't see the roads outside for all the precipitation. I bought myself a wrap, sat down, looked outside and thought to myself: "This is just daft. To come up this way in this weather was a stupid idea."

I turned around to watch a cleaner come up to my table

in the corner and place a yellow 'Caution - Wet Floor' sign on the floor in front of me. Then I looked down to see that I was so wet that I had dripped a trail of water from the front door to the counter when I got served, and then to my table where I'd sat down. I'd now been at the table so long that a puddle had formed underneath me, big enough for the McDonald's staff to have concerns from a health and safety viewpoint.

I sat at the table, still feeling despondent, got out my phone and logged onto my Facebook account. Now that I was becoming more of a cult figure around Dons fans, more of them started to think of me and what I was going through in such foul weather. My Facebook wall was inundated with messages of support, most of them along the lines of: "We think you're a bloody idiot, but keep going!" That gave me the resolve to make the McDonald's cleaners' lives a bit easier and get the last 20 miles out of the way.

It was noon when I left McDonald's, and half an hour later I'd completed around ten of those 20 miles when my phone rang. It was Margaret. The inevitable that had been hanging over me all morning (aside from rain clouds) had been confirmed. The Keepmoat pitch had taken in just too much water. The game had been postponed. Margaret was on the supporters' coach, with Dan, Ross and the rest of the away regulars gang, and she was at Tibshelf services on the M1, only around 20 miles south of Doncaster, when she got the call. To add to my problems, she told me that the coach was turning round and heading straight back to Milton Keynes, along with all the clothes I needed to get changed into.

This put me into a sort of survival mode. I resolved to ride up to Doncaster, stop at a sports shop, buy a tracksuit with my credit card to give me something dry and warm to wear, and then get the train home, however long it took. I rode another five miles until I was just outside Doncaster, when my phone rang again. John Cove was on the line and told me he'd given my mobile number to Damien Doyle, the Dons' sports science guru. Then Nicola rang, to say she would pick me up and that I wasn't to panic. Then Damien rang and said that the team coach was also happy to wait for me and that I could come back with the squad. I was pretty torn on this one as Nicola had offered to pick me up. I asked Damien if they had any spare clothes. As they didn't, I refused their offer: the right thing to do as I was still about 20 minutes away and I didn't want to hold them up.

When I reached the Keepmoat Stadium, it was deserted. There were barely any cars around, and the only doors that were open were to the box office and the club reception. I'd originally arranged to meet Charles Swallow, Rovers' customer services manager, when I arrived, so I went to sit in reception more in hope than expectation that he would still be around. The receptionist went to check and it transpired that Charles had actually waited for me to arrive to get me sorted. He took me inside so I could get showered, and then a woman came from nowhere and offered me a cup of tea. I told her that would be lovely, and she disappeared to get that sorted. A few minutes later, Nicola arrived and Charles took her on a tour of the stadium while I showered and changed into some Doncaster Rovers training kit that had been sorted for me.

It was just as well that Nicola had arrived because as we all sat in the groundstaff restroom, the lady came back with pots of tea and about ten enormous hot steak pies in proper earthenware pie dishes. It was amazing. I devoured my pie like I imagine Oliver Twist would have devoured a second bowl of gruel, had Mr Bumble been a tad more flush with the servings. We were immensely grateful for this typical Yorkshire show of hospitality - there's nothing in t'world that can't be fixed with a pot o' tea and a steak pie! Doncaster Rovers will now always remain close to my heart.

As we left, we took a look at the pitch to find that the

rain had stopped and that the pitch had drained sufficiently for the game to go ahead, in my mind at least. Obviously the referee had to make the call to postpone it on the weather he was facing at the time, and the players wouldn't have been able to warm up on it (I was looking at it just before 3:00), so it remained the right decision, albeit a frustrating one. But even without the game, I still regard that day as a rewarding day out – the ride was a triumph over adversity, it was another long-distance ride ticked off (there was no need for me to do Doncaster again now that I'd done it once), and the warm welcome from the Rovers staff had lifted my spirits markedly. As Nicola drove me back home, I felt it was a positive way to finish 2012 and effectively reach the halfway point of the season.

Christmas and New Year were both quiet, pleasant affairs in the Faiers household, but the festive period was punctuated by a week of absolute disasters for the Dons on the pitch. We'd managed to keep ourselves around the play-off places, despite the odd wobble, but the biggest hammer blow of the whole season came the day before Christmas Eve, when it was announced that our two best players had been injured in training. Luke Chadwick had done his knee ligaments while Stephen Gleeson had broken his left foot. Both would be out for two months at least. The pair were the heart and soul of our midfield, and on a limited budget, there was no way Robinson would be able to fully replace them in the January transfer window.

The absence of Chadwick and Gleeson, and how it weakened our team as a whole, was apparent immediately. We had two home games between Christmas and New Year, in which our previously excellent home record was blown apart by defeats to Walsall (4-2) and Coventry (3-2). All of a sudden, even reaching the play-offs was starting to look like a struggle, and having only won three away games in the league thus far, picking up more points on our travels would become essential over the remaining four months of the season.

STADIUM CHASE

With a trip to Nottingham and Notts County's Meadow Lane scheduled for January 1, the year 2013 started very, very early for me. Thankfully, Margaret and I aren't the type to go overboard on New Year's Eve, so it was no problem for me to get myself out of bed and up to Milton Keynes for a 9:00am start. I was hoping that my journey north would again be eased by the huge tailwind that I benefitted from en route to Doncaster ten days previously, but there had been a major weather system change over Christmas. Now the prevailing winds were blowing to the south, which meant every ride to a ground north of MK required me to push into a headwind. This was to last for most of the rest of the season.

At 80 miles, Nottingham isn't too far from Milton Keynes in the grand scheme of things, meaning the ride shouldn't have been too much of a problem, and I had extra motivation to get there so I could meet up with a couple of old County-supporting friends. But the wind made the whole ride an absolute chore. I stopped at my usual rest point in Oakham, which was just over halfway to Nottingham, absolutely staggered at how much energy I'd had to expend just to get to ruddy Rutland. It didn't get any easier once I resumed either: it was a constant grind and push against the force of the wind all the way to Nottingham. As I finished, I met up with my friend Alastair and we were taken pitchside for pictures. Alastair's son James was instrumental in getting me lots of coverage in Nottingham after the game and Notts County themselves were really generous in donating some match tickets for me to raffle off for the cause.

Despite my assurances to Alastair that Notts would easily win, Daniel Powell and Darren Potter put us 2-0 up inside 15 minutes, and despite County getting one back with a penalty early in the second half, we held on for a crucial away win. The ride home on the coach was a fun one.

Four days later, I was headed north again, as we faced

Championship side Sheffield Wednesday in the third round of the FA Cup at Hillsborough. What could have been a real arduous ride up was made a lot easier by two things: one was the weather on the day (dry, sunny, not too cold, only a slight headwind) and also by my physical condition. The run of rides had been relatively quiet for me since late November, and that had given me some downtime to recover and get back into peak shape. The Notts County ride was perfectly placed before the trip to Sheffield, because 80 miles was an ideal distance to get back into the swing of things and ease myself into long-haul riding once again.

It was another early start – about 5:30am – and despite the fact that Sheffield is pretty close to Doncaster, I'd opted to take the Peak District route once again. Much of it was the same as my two-day ride to Preston in October, through Hinckley and up to Derby. In October, I had felt very low approaching Derby so I was looking forward to seeing how I would fare this time. After the usual run north on the A5, I was this time met by my friend Chris in Burbage, near Hinckley. With Chris living in Rugby, this was the start of some incredibly useful support that he gave me over the course of the following few months. Professional cycling teams have 'soigneurs' – the guys who do massages, hand out musettes (bags) of food during the race, and generally ensure the riders are happy. Chris became my soigneur that day (bar the massage) and continued throughout the project to give some of the best support a friend could ever give.

I carried on from Hinckley, past the bench where I'd had a bit of a cry earlier in the season, and arrived at Derby in really good time. I knew I needed to get onto the A38 to carry on around the east of the Peak District, but due to the strange signposting in Derby and ridiculous one-way system, I was headed out of the town in the wrong direction. I looked at the map and the only way to rectify the situation was an evil-looking climb over a hill called

Duffield Bank. This was going to be interesting. I steeled myself as the climb started and despite an initial trepidation, I felt some satisfaction climbing it at a fair speed. This was my first proper hill since the Preston ride and it told me that my internal motor was well and truly running again after the relatively quiet end to 2012.

Dropping down the other side, I found my correct route but took the wrong turn again, running up onto the A38 trunk road. This was a busy dual carriageway that my mum wouldn't have approved of, but I was going well and I knew that it would shave a few miles off the next section of the route to Chesterfield, the next town I needed to reach. I figured that early on a Saturday morning it would still be pretty quiet, despite being a major route, but it turned out to be teeming with weekend traffic once I'd got on it. I battled for my space with the traffic, which proved a little stressful at times, but the shortcut worked: by the time I reached Chesterfield, it was just gone noon and I had plenty of time to complete the last short section through Sheffield to Hillsborough.

I felt pleased with myself as I arrived in Chesterfield. It had taken me six and a half hours to complete 110 miles, including a food stop and some very hilly terrain. As a sporting cyclist, I felt it was one of my best performances of the season. I gave myself a pat on the back for this by stopping for an ice-cream at McDonald's in town (I had time in hand to do so), and while I was there, I got talking to a couple of local policemen. It turned out they were both Wednesday fans who were going to the game that afternoon, and after I explained who I was and the ride I was doing, they half-jokingly offered to give me a blues-and-twos escort all the way to Hillsborough. As cool as that would have been, I thought that might have been pushing things a little bit too far, so I declined. Later I found out that the Dons supporters' coaches had received their own police escort to the ground – the only time all season this happened. "I knew South Yorkshire Police were hot on escorting away fans, but covering one lone cyclist is ridiculous!" I mused.

Copper-less, I sped along the A61, entering Sheffield from the south. I wasn't entirely sure of the way through the city centre to Hillsborough, which is located in the north-west outskirts of the 'Steel City'. As had become traditional when I'd got lost in towns, I asked a moped rider for directions while we waited at some traffic lights. He told me he was going there himself, and he gave me directions. We set off, and clearly he wasn't expecting me to be able to keep up with him, so when he turned round and saw me at the next lights, he said: "You might as well just follow me, then."

A few minutes later, he delivered me at Hillsborough. I'd told Margaret I'd meet her by the memorial by the main entrance, which remembers the lives of the 96 Liverpool fans that so tragically lost their lives there in 1989. She wasn't around, so I went into the reception, and took advantage of the shower and changing facilities Wednesday had so kindly offered, along with a signed shirt for the cause that I could put into my raffle. Then I got my bike stowed into Nicola's car (she and Margaret had arrived by then), walked around to the away end turnstiles and was greeted by one of the nicest surprises I'd ever had in my life.

As I've mentioned previously, the reaction of Dons fans to my project had been a little lukewarm to begin with. As such, getting donations to come in had proved more difficult than I'd hoped, although I'd already managed to pass my initial target of raising £1000 by the time I'd travelled to Hillsborough. But the story of my ride to Doncaster two weeks previously for the game that never was, through all the incredibly bad weather, had spread like wildfire through the stands at stadium:mk. At the two home games over Christmas, people I barely knew or didn't know at all were coming up to give me their congratulations/sympathy for the Doncaster ride. I thought it was all lovely at the time, but it didn't seem to be translating into donations.

That all changed at Hillsborough, thanks to the efforts of Clarkie and Dawn, a lovely couple that travel to most of the Dons' away games. On the morning of the game, they organised a giant whip-round for my fund on all nine coaches that travelled up from MK. With every one of those coaches packed, that meant they'd solicited donations from just over 450 people. So imagine the look on my face when they came up to me outside the ground and presented me with a Jiffy bag containing around £750.

I was flabbergasted. They'd added around 50 per cent to my fund for the entire season in one morning of collections. They'd managed to connect with a big chunk of our fanbase to help me out, entirely on their own initiative, without asking or telling me about it, and with nothing in it for them. I genuinely didn't know how to thank them. And having completed one of my most 'competitive' rides of the season, I was on cloud nine.

And so, it seems, were the other 1200 Dons fans that had come up to Hillsborough. There were balloons and the like, and everyone was in an 'FA Cup run, no League pressure, let's enjoy this, nothing to lose' kind of mood. And we were really loud that day. Being honest, it's not often you say that about MK Dons fans, but we made an absolute racket. I'm still sure that it made a difference to the performance of the team, who made a team from the division above look like a bunch of amateurs.

How we didn't score that day is still genuinely beyond me. The game finished goalless, but an even better performance at home in the replay ten days later earned us a 2-0 win and a fourth-round game – our first-ever FA Cup fourth-round game – away at Queens Park Rangers (another ride onto the list). With the Rs at the bottom of the Premier League, with Harry Redknapp newly appointed as manager and with QPR being the team that knocked us out of the Cup a year previously, the prospect was mouth-watering. Everything was set up for a giant-killing at Loftus Road.

Prior to the QPR game on January 26, we had one League away fixture scheduled, at Crewe Alexandra the Saturday before. But then the snow came. I'd been able to do a week of local training after the game at Hillsborough, but then the white stuff came falling to the ground in the week leading up to the Crewe fixture and it became impossible for me to get out on the bike at all. Unlike the Doncaster game, there was no uncertainty about whether this game was going to go ahead or not, and all I wanted was the confirmation of the postponement to come through reasonably early, so at least I hadn't tried to get up there. Sure enough, at 11:30am the day before the game, it was called off. Good news for me, as it kept me out of the snow, but bad news for me and my new employer (I'd changed jobs in November) – I'd have to send in another application for a Tuesday off at some point…

A few days later, the weather improved, which was a boost to my confidence for the rides ahead. Getting to QPR didn't bother me – a simple ride to West London was chump-change to me by that stage, and London is habitually warmer than other parts of the country, thereby reducing the risk of snow and ice. What was worrying me was the trek to deepest, darkest Somerset the following Tuesday. Our game at Yeovil Town had been shunted back from its original date, as we were up in Yorkshire that day playing Sheffield Wednesday.

This was the problem with committing to do every single game: I was at the complete mercy of the weather on the day, and there was no backing out of anything. Mindful that a one-day ride to Yeovil in sub-zero temperatures could cause me some real problems, I went on the blag, ringing the likes of Trek and other bike companies to try and get myself kitted out in some winter gear in exchange for a bit of charity-related publicity. I tried to get hold of a cross-country bike (bigger, thicker wheels to clear snow, and other modifications – if you imagine a road racing bike is a Formula 1 car, then a cross-country bike is like a rally car). That effort, unsurprisingly, came up with nothing, but it was worth a try. I didn't have any money myself to get some winter gear, so I pinned my hopes on the weather and hoped that it would improve.

In the meantime, the ride to QPR caused me no problems, as expected, and Dons fans were coming down mob-handed for the next chapter of our amazing FA Cup run. We'd sold out Loftus Road's away end, meaning more than 3100 Dons fans would be in attendance: our biggest-ever away following, excluding the trip to Wembley for the Johnstone's Paint Trophy final in 2008. There were more than 20 coaches coming down from stadium:mk, and I rode down South Africa Road, past the main entrance to the stadium, just as the coaches were emptying out.

As awareness of me had improved after the Doncaster trip and the Hillsborough collection, no-one was in any doubt as to who I was: there was applause, cheering and all sorts of well-wishers. It was another sign that what I was doing was really starting to make a difference. In retrospect, my only regret is that I didn't get this kind of attention much earlier in the season. Not because I wanted it for the ego boost – I don't consider myself to be that kind of person – but because it could have generated substantially more money for the fund, which was the whole purpose of the project in the first place. There are other things in long-distance cycling I have planned for the future, and I know that the lessons I've learned with this adventure will prove extremely useful when it comes to planning those.

And then, as if my day couldn't get any better, there was the game itself. If I thought the match at Hillsborough had been good, this was sublime. QPR weren't fielding their first XI, although the team Redknapp had put out still contained seven internationals, and names like Rob Green, Anton Ferdinand, Tal Ben Haim, Fabio da Silva and DJ

Campbell were of a status way above those we had on the field, especially with Chadwick and Gleeson still missing. When Campbell had a goal disallowed after 45 seconds, things looked bleak, but soon after, the Dons got a corner. I couldn't tell who headed the ball (it turned out later it was Armand Traore past his own keeper), but all I could make out was a ball hitting a net and Lewington wheeling away in celebration. Four minutes in and we were beating a Premier League team at a Premier League ground. I couldn't believe it.

QPR dominated possession in the early stages but couldn't make a breakthrough, and were clearly getting frustrated at how they couldn't dispatch the League One minnows. Then a long ball launched forward, Ferdinand missed it and Ryan Lowe coolly slotted it past Green. 2-0. This was incredible.

I expected a QPR onslaught after half-time, but it didn't come. Quite the reverse, in fact: their players started arguing amongst themselves, and the Dons ripped them to shreds. First Lowe recovered a ball that was seemingly going out on the dead-ball line, and crossed in for loanee Ryan Harley to tap in for 3-0. And then, as the ball bobbled around the box, Darren Potter steered the ball into the far corner for 4-0 after just 56 minutes.

The Dons fans were delirious. I spotted the lads with the drum going absolutely bananas. I spotted Dan, tears in his eyes, topless on a cold January day, waving his shirt round and round his head. I spotted thousands of QPR fans ranting and raving at the hapless Hoops on the field and streaming for the exits with more than half an hour still to go. It was absolute heaven. Even the two consolation goals the Rs scored late on couldn't put a dampener on proceedings. I found out later that some QPR fans on one of their internet forums had voted the defeat as the biggest embarrassment in the club's history, even bigger than when they were knocked out of the Cup by Vauxhall Motors. I felt the exact opposite. On that day,

STADIUM CHASE

perhaps more than any other, I was proud and excited to be an MK Dons fan.

CHAPTER 6: FROM YEOVIL TO AUCKLAND

The short coach journey back from QPR was fantastic. Despite the game and the result they'd just seen, people just wanted to talk to me about cycling. They wanted to know all about what I was doing: how things had gone so far, which rides I'd found the toughest and, most often, how I was going to manage Carlisle. At 265 miles and two very hard days, the trip to Carlisle United was the longest of the lot, and by this stage it was only four weeks away.

I had a massive month coming. I had the ride to Carlisle, and on top of that I had to travel to New Zealand for work – I would miss the away game at Oldham on February 9, but I resolved to ride the equivalent mileage while I was out there. The logistics of taking a bike down there with me was taking up a lot of my time, but before that, the next big hairy monster on the horizon was a ride to Yeovil.

Once I got home from Loftus Road, I checked the weather for the ride to Yeovil about every two hours, right up until I left for Somerset first thing Tuesday morning (January 29). The tiny numbers indicating the temperature in degrees Celsius didn't bother me. What did bother me was the black circle below with an arrow protruding from it with the number '22' in the middle, taunting me. I really wasn't looking forward to trying to ride all that way through a 22mph headwind.

Knowing that the weather would be bad, I spent a lot of time trying to get hold of Yeovil Town to arrange somewhere to change. They weren't too bothered about helping me out, and told me I could get changed in the gents toilet in the away end. For anyone who has been to Yeovil, the gents loos are not the biggest and what I really wanted was something that was warm, with hot water if possible. Not for the first time, Paul Heald, ex-Wimbledon goalkeeper and MK Dons goalkeeping coach, came to the rescue and arranged for me to use the first-team changing room as long as I reached Huish Park by 6:00pm. Further to that, England and Somerset cricketer James Hildreth, who is a big MK Dons fan, said he would meet me when I arrived. This was a great offer and would really help to increase the profile of the project. So all of a sudden, I was on a deadline.

There are so many things that made that day probably my worst of the whole season, irrespective of what happened before or what was to happen after. To save me an extra bit of mileage, Margaret packed my stuff and my bike into the car and drove me to stadium:mk. I would usually have cycled up to the stadium, so while I was getting my bike out the car, the realisation that I had left my helmet at home made my heart sink. We had to go back and pick it up. The traffic was awful and by the time we got back to my house, I was an hour and a half behind schedule, so I decided to leave for Yeovil straight from my house. Without looking at the route to see if any changes would benefit me, I headed off and tried to make up some time.

Right from the off, the wind was just dreadful, even during the first section west to Bicester. The wind was blowing from the south-west, exactly the direction I was travelling in, which meant a headwind all the way, or a bitter crosswind on any sections of the route that were winding rather than direct. But I tried to work through that and push on through.

I circumnavigated Oxford and carried on towards Witney, a stretch punctuated by a seemingly endless stream of phonecalls. Some of them were from BBC Radio

Somerset, who had picked up on my story and wanted to arrange an interview for later on, and some of them were work phonecalls that I was just unable to divert, what with it being a Tuesday. Every time my phone rang, I had to stop, fish my phone out of my bike bag, take the call, put it back and then carry on, an incredible faff that became a real irritant after the fourth or fifth call as it chewed up even more of my time.

Eventually I reached Witney, and came up to a confusing roundabout for which I wasn't sure of which lane I should be in. As I lined up in the left-hand lane, a bus pulled hard left, right across in front of me to block the whole road, and the female driver then got out of her seat and made to get off the bus and give me an earful. I wasn't sure exactly what I did wrong to earn her ire, and quite frankly, I didn't care (still don't). I had to get to Yeovil and time was ticking on, so before she had a chance to get off the bus, I rode away and got on with it.

From Witney, I travelled due south towards Swindon, and from then on it was *really* hard going. It had started to rain with gradually increasing intensity, and you could see a huge belt of heavy rainfall in the general direction I was headed. The wind had also picked up yet further, and this just added to my misery. I was so far behind schedule, I chose not to stop for food or hot drinks and ploughed on. This was the wrong decision and just after Witney, I started to feel really hungry. It was a thoroughly miserable experience. I wanted to be anywhere else but on a bike. If I could have been on a packed London Underground train in rush hour with my face wedged up a fat bloke's armpit, I'd have taken it.

I stopped at a Co-op (because it was all I could find) and grabbed some supplies for lunch, just before I got into Swindon. There was nowhere to sit outside, so I sat on the footpath, in the cold and wet, with no shelter. The influx of food into my system did little to ease my misery. I remounted, rode past Swindon and over the M4, and as I rode onto Salisbury Plain, the lack of any cover from the wind meant I was constantly being blown backwards. What had initially been difficult was becoming impossible.

Not only was the wind itself blowing strongly, but there were also gusts which made it supremely difficult to maintain a regular rhythm on the pedals. I was on a single-carriageway road with a raised verge, which meant there was no way I could keep myself well to one side, and this A-road was choked with lorries and tankers in both directions, meaning there was precious little room for error. The spray from those lorries was soaking me even more, and making me feel cold right down to the bone.

Then the southbound road turned right and started to head west, turning that headwind into a powerful crosswind. It's never easy for a cyclist to keep themselves in a straight line in a crosswind, and the gusts that day were so strong that I was frequently getting blown into the middle of the road. I'm not a person who shies away from a challenge, but this was too much, even for me. This was getting dangerous. It would only take one badly-timed gust and one lorry coming up behind me and I was toast.

It probably would have been better for me to think through what I was doing and change my route, rather than pig-headedly continue to plough my way across Salisbury Plain. If I'd done that, I certainly could have got a lot further, and would have stood a much better chance of reaching Yeovil, and doing so in time for the 7:45pm kick-off. But everything that had already happened to me that day meant that I simply wasn't thinking straight. With darkness approaching, I decided that this was just silly, and that no-one was going to think any less of me if I just stopped.

I got into a village and decided to ring Margaret and Nicola to get them to pick me up on their way to Yeovil. I wasn't too far off the route they would have taken to drive there. I tried to find a pub to get some shelter, but strangely all the pubs in this village seemed to have shut down. So I had to carry on another five miles into Avebury, and found a pub in which to raise the white flag and surrender. I'd given it my best, but I'd failed.

With no signal, the landlord sympathetically lent me the pub's phone to call from and a quick conversation with Nicola sorted out the arrangements for her to pick me up. At that time (3:00), and because of the forced rapidity of the call, I didn't realise that Nicola was stuck in traffic..

At 6:00, my rescuers arrived, having suffered continuously heavy traffic. We loaded the car and headed off to Yeovil. Nicola then had to endure even more dreadful traffic to get us to the ground and we arrived just five minutes before kick-off. En route, I conducted my interview with BBC Radio Somerset by phone, during which I got to detail my failure in all its glory. The presenter sounded sympathetic to my plight, bless him.

Once I did get to Huish Park, I found Hildreth waiting outside in the pouring rain, having hung around for me, and we enjoyed a cup of tea alongside the first few minutes of the game. The match imitated my day perfectly: we lost 2-1 as Yeovil continued their incredible run of winter form that had sent them rocketing up the League One table and right into the promotion race.

Of course, my failure to arrive before the deadline of 6pm meant that even though I was cold and badly in need of a change, I had to resort to getting changed in the gents loo after all, which I did as the other Dons fans that made the trip (99 of us in all, in stark contrast to the QPR game) came streaming in and out for a pre-game leak. To be honest, by that time I was beyond caring and the sight of me getting changed in practically the open air just made more fans appreciative of the scale of what I was trying to do.

Come the end of the game, I was hoping to meet one of Yeovil's staff, who had promised that I'd be able to get a picture while I was there, and maybe even some memorabilia to add to the raffle collection. I went round to the club reception, but even as late as 10:30pm, some 50 minutes after the game had finished, he hadn't come down and they were still messing me about. Eventually, I did get a picture, and he told me to send him an email about memorabilia and that they'd stick something in the post. Given everything I've already described to you about this thoroughly awful day, dear reader, it will probably surprise you not a jot to hear that they never did send anything through to me.

There remains unfinished business for me with Yeovil, because I still want to follow up on my promise and complete a ride down there for a game with them. Next time we play away at Yeovil, I'll be attempting it again. I may have to wait a while for that, as Yeovil's late-season charge for promotion to the Championship proved to be a successful one, but I'm not going to be forgetting about this in a hurry. I will do that ride one day (weather permitting, obviously!).

As an eventful month of January drew to a close, I really needed a pick-me-up. And going to New Zealand on a paid-for work trip is a damned good one. My job requires me to travel abroad now and again, and well in advance, I knew that in early February, I would have to spend two weeks in Auckland. It was clear when I started all this that I was going to have to miss a ride while I was away, and given that I had a certain degree of choice as to when I was going to travel, early February seemed like the best time. I would only miss the away game at Oldham Athletic on February 9, a ride I'd effectively already done by travelling to Bury a few miles up the road back in September.

I should clarify at this point that I have nothing against Oldham. A few friends had teased me, saying that the reason I chose that game to skip was because Oldham is 'not the nicest place in the world to visit' (a polite way of putting the eight-letter word starting with S that most people used to describe the town). But that wasn't the case: it was just the most convenient part of the calendar for me to travel, both in terms of the fixture list and my family life. The fact that the Dons went up to Boundary Park that day and lost 3-1 in a match Dan later described as 'our worst performance of the entire season' was entirely coincidental.

As I mentioned earlier, I intended to cycle the equivalent Oldham distance while I was away, and packing my bike up to get it checked into the plane's hold was a new experience for me. My bike was dismantled and put into a bike box, which is around 1.5 times the size of a regular large suitcase, after which the airline is simply able to treat it as a regular piece of luggage. I was flying premium economy with Air New Zealand, which allowed each piece of luggage to weigh in at a maximum of 23kg. With my bike being a carbon-framed lightweight racer, this wasn't anywhere near being a problem.

The tricky bit was actually just getting it to Heathrow in the first place. Once you've got it packed up, you don't have to worry about it, but taking off handlebars, pedals and so on and fitting them into a limited space wasn't easy. It was similar to attempting a 3D jigsaw puzzle - putting one item in one place had implications for other bits on the other side. It took me about two hours the first time I packed it up, but once I'd found a layout that worked, it was easy to do it again for the flight home.

I was a little nervous about handing the case over at check-in, given the occasional habit for airlines to lose luggage. Once I had been through the security checks (a process that I can only imagine is similar to what cattle go through at the abattoir), I was able to watch the luggage being loaded onto the aeroplane from the waiting area. The fact I couldn't see my pride and joy being loaded kept me on edge for the entire 24-hour flight. I had visions of it being left behind in a nondescript box on the tarmac in West London and consequently being snaffled away and sold at a car boot sale in Uxbridge. When I arrived in

STADIUM CHASE

Auckland to collect the bike box from the oversize luggage area, it was the very last item to come out, giving me a few extra nail-biting minutes as I waited for what I thought would be the confirmation that my bike and I were 12,000 miles apart. But Air New Zealand had everything working like clockwork, so I needn't have worried.

As I reached my short-stay apartment, in the shadow of Mount Eden and a stone's throw from the Eden Park stadium, I felt relaxed in the warm late-summer Antipodean climate, but very lethargic having spent 24 hours crammed into a plane seat. Yes, I was in premium economy, and yes, Air New Zealand is one of the better airlines with which to fly long-haul, but it's still 24 hours on a plane. So the first thing I did once I'd dumped my suitcase and showered was to open up the bike box, put my bike back together and head straight out to explore Auckland.

I wanted to make the most of having my bike out there, so before I left England I got in touch with a few local bike clubs in the Auckland area, to see if I could tag along with them for any longer, more challenging rides. I quickly found that bike clubs in New Zealand had a very different way of doing things: whereas British clubs would meet for rides at evenings and weekends, Kiwi clubs would meet up at 6:30am on weekday mornings and put a good 40 miles in before heading off to work.

That didn't faze me, but it soon transpired that even my high level of fitness wasn't good enough for these guys: as it was late summer down there, it was coming towards the end of their cycling season and all the riders were therefore at the peak of their performance. While I wasn't exactly out of shape, my long-distance treks to away games made me what cyclists refer to as a 'diesel engine': someone who can keep going for mile after mile, but can't produce any devastating bursts of acceleration. After all, I had no need to launch any attacks up mountains while riding to football games because I was the only one there.

But I digress. I did my best to keep up with the locals, but it wasn't really working.

The middle Saturday of my trip was the day of the Oldham game, and so I planned to take in a 152-mile ride starting and finishing at my apartment in Auckland to replicate the distance I would have ridden to Greater Manchester. I visited the local bike shop the day before to ask the aficionados there for route advice, because I wanted something that would give me a proper challenge. The route I chose eventually was to take the ferry out of Auckland across the harbour. From there, I would take the road north to the seaside town of Whangaparoah and then ride west, inland to Helensville. That route wrote itself as the New Zealand road network is very different from that of the UK: because of the landscape and the fact that there are more sheep than people, there is often only one road into a town. A place I really wanted to go on the route back into Auckland was Bethells Beach but there was just one spur road from the main road there and back. This would add 40 miles, but I was assured it was a beautiful place.

After that diversion, I would have to return to the main road and head back to Auckland up some serious climbs over the Waitekeres, a series of mountains to the west of the city. A major plus point was that the trip coincided with the start of the England cricket tour, so I was able to finish at England's first T20 international against New Zealand at Eden Park.

I started at about 6:30am on the warm, sunny Saturday morning (when it was still Friday evening back in the UK) knowing I had to be back by 4pm to get ready for the cricket match. With the addition of the spur to Bethells Beach, the distance was nearer 160 miles so although it would be tough, it was certainly achievable. I sped down to the ferry terminal to find I'd just missed the ferry I'd wanted to catch, and so had to wait an hour for the next one. This made timings slightly tighter but I was still confident I'd make Eden Park for the toss. Eventually I was deposited on the other side of the water and onto the main road heading north. It was 7:30am, the sun was warming North Island and the roads were quiet.

I carried on with ease and came to a pleasant little café to stop for breakfast. I sat out at the roadside as the weather was so good, and saw a cycle club ride up the road towards me. As a fellow cyclist, I thought I'd wave and acknowledge them, but not a single one of them made any gesture towards me. They just looked straight ahead and carried on up the road. This wasn't the only time this happened on the trip, either – I found most Kiwi cyclists to be very insular and aloof, something that was completely at odds with the kinship that is part and parcel of cycling culture in Europe.

After I resumed, I happily munched up the miles until I reached the town of Whangaparoah. The town sits on a peninsula, and my route took me to the end of it before I turned towards Helensville. I came across a beautiful beach, by which there was a couple sitting on a bench enjoying the view, so I asked them if they'd take my picture. We stopped and chatted for a few minutes, and it turned out that they were Australian. Football is getting big in Australia and they knew a lot about the English leagues – it's an international language these days – so we had plenty to chat about. As I headed back inland, I looked back on my previous ride to a game, to Yeovil, and felt so much better that I was riding a bike in a temperature above five degrees Celsius and I wasn't being blown all over Salisbury Plain. To celebrate the fact, I stopped at a small shop and bought an ice cream. I certainly wouldn't have done that if I was riding to Oldham!

It was the next section to Helensville that gave me some cause for concern. The roads were covered in loose tarmac chippings that I feared would give me a puncture, but thankfully I got away without getting a flat. That section turned out to be particularly enjoyable, with long, straight roads that stretched up to the horizon. It was 1:00pm by the time I reached Helensville, and I had to make a choice; the spur to Bethells Beach was going to add too much time, so I chose to return the next day and do that separately. Decision made, I had three hours to go to complete 40 miles. I felt comfortable for time, even though I'd have to traverse the Waitekeres.

My Garmin had suggested that the climbs and descents of the Waitekeres were going to be big. As I rode nearer, they loomed large and as I passed through the village that the hills are named after, the realisation of how big they were finally dawned. There is a main road that runs up to, and along the ridgeline, called Scenic Drive. It's a pleasant-sounding name, but it belied the absolute hell I was about to put myself through.

I turned right onto Scenic Drive and the road just went *up*. It was a series of tight corners, not dissimilar to an alpine road and certainly nothing like my regular encounters on the roads of sunny Milton Keynes. I was in my smallest gear and turning a reasonable pace but after about 30 minutes of this, I was starting to fall apart. My breathing was fast and I felt like I could hear every vein in my body bursting. I just wasn't prepared for how big and tough this was going to be. The 100 miles I had already travelled didn't really help, either. The road didn't relent one bit. Finally, I reached a crest and was able to enjoy a few minutes of freewheeling. My mind was playing tricks and I convinced myself that I had finished the climb. No such luck as the next corner revealed more uphill battles. Three times I crested the hills and each time, my hopes that it was over were cruelly dashed.

After 13 agonising miles, I reached a viewpoint with a bench and pulled over to sit down. I was completely spent: I had run out of water but worse still, I was getting very hungry. I even tore open my used energy gel packets to lick the insides clean, so desperate was I for calories. It was the longest climb I'd ever done. As I sat there, looking over Auckland, a car pulled up and the two occupants smiled and waved a hello. I didn't know how much more of this ridge I could take and I asked if they knew of a café nearby. If this had been England, there would have been a Starbucks at the viewpoint, but I think the Kiwis take a dim view of that sort of thing. They looked kindly and said they didn't know, but really generously and without prompting, came over and said: "You've run out of water, have this. We saw you on the road and noticed that your bottle was empty." I couldn't believe it. They had actually turned back to give me a drink. It goes to show how people can conspire to ensure you succeed. I was very grateful.

I headed off, and my fears of more climbing were soon allayed. The road started going downhill and despite one or two more short uphill sections, I was definitively headed back to sea-level. I was still desperately hungry, though, and thankfully, as I started to fizzle out a small roadside restaurant revealed itself around the next corner. Getting off my bike, I walked in to find it was a trendy jazz bar with lots of city-types enjoying the first-class views from the verandah. Feeling somewhat out of place in my sweaty lycra, I walked up to the bar. I couldn't afford a club sandwich, so said to the barman (in a style resembling a spaghetti western) 'Coke – the biggest you've got.' Two minutes and one litre of fizzy stuff later, I told the barman what I was doing. Needless to say, he thought I was an idiot, but we chatted for a minute. He reassured me I was only about 12 miles from home and it would all be downhill.

I climbed back onto the bike and within a few minutes discovered that the descent at this end of the range wasn't particularly steady or relaxing. It was, in fact, akin to speeding down the side of an Alp. For three miles, I hurtled down the mountain, leaning into corners like Valentino Rossi. It was descending at an intensity I'd never experienced before. It was far too fast for me to touch the brakes: all I could do to slow down for corners was to sit up and use my body as a big sail and let the air resistance bring me back down to vaguely sane speeds. The roads levelled out as I reached Auckland and with time against me, I time-trialled the final part. I even managed to climb the short hill up to Ponsonby (the area I was staying in) in one of the fastest times the road has ever been cycled, according to the Strava website that logged all my Garmin data. I had 20 minutes to shower, change and eat as much as I could before my friends from work collected me to go to the cricket. England then won, which capped off a truly unforgettable day.

The next day, I lazed around the apartment and decided that I would finish my riding off in the evening as the temperature had soared to 30 degrees. I rode back to the Waitekere mountains but thankfully only skirted the lower foothills on my way back to Bethells Beach. The road out of Auckland took me into what looked like a rainforest: dense woodland covering a wide, sweeping road completely devoid of traffic. Cruising along in the warm evening sun, this was heaven. Uphill or downhill, it didn't matter – it was magical. As I escaped from the forest, and rode in between two mountains and passed through the gateway, the deep blue ocean burst into view, with black, volcanic sand lining the coast.

I found a small shack that turned out to be a café and so treated myself to the usual Coke and ice-cream and sat down to take in the view. I got talking to an English woman and her boyfriend at the next table, who had just moved out to New Zealand. We talked about my challenge, at which point she casually dropped into the conversation that she was from Carlisle.

That awoke me from the dream that had been New Zealand. The trip to Carlisle, the Big One, was now my next ride, and less than two weeks away. I reflected on the road back home that the arduous climbs around New Zealand had inadvertently become my training camp for

Carlisle. I was as ready for Carlisle as I was ever going to be. Little did I know that to get there, I was going to have to push my body and my mind further than I ever had before.

CHAPTER 7: CARLISLE

Come the Tuesday after Oldham (February 12), I was still in New Zealand and therefore missed the rearranged away game at Doncaster that had so cruelly been postponed as I reached the Keepmoat Stadium just before Christmas. As I'd completed the ride there the first time round, I decided there wasn't any need for me to do it again – and no, I still don't think that's cheating!

It was Wednesday morning local time for me when the game took place as NZ was 13 hours ahead of the UK, but I was at work and so unable to access the online Dons Player to listen to the live commentary. That left me with the BBC Sport website, watching morsels of information flicker up on my screen every time I nervously jabbed at the Refresh key. It felt thoroughly odd knowing a Dons game was going on that I wasn't at, and equally odd checking the updates at 10:00 on a Wednesday morning. It reminded me of dragging myself out of bed to sit in front of the TV and watch all those early morning games in the 2002 World Cup.

The game remained goalless and with about 15 minutes to go, I began to think that we'd do what countless other away teams have done in the past and lose 1-0 thanks to a home team putting in a grandstand finish. It finished 0-0, still leaving the Dons a long way off that elusive play-off zone and leaving me frustrated that we hadn't picked up the league win that had escaped our grasp since New Year's Day. Come full-time, I was left feeling flat as a pancake (which was somewhat apt as it was Shrove Tuesday in the UK), but hardly the best feeling in the world when you still have a full day's work ahead of you...

If Doncaster had pinched the win, I wouldn't have held any grudges, given the fantastic treatment they'd affored me when I'd cycled up for the postponed original fixture seven weeks previously. Margaret went to the rearranged game and reported back that the club's fans and their customer services manager Charlie Swallow had been fantastically helpful for me. He gave her that night's match programme, which contained a big piece on my project, which I thought was a really nice touch.

I left Auckland to fly back to London the following Saturday (February 16), the day on which the Dons played their first-ever FA Cup fifth-round game, at home against Barnsley. Being on the plane and disconnected from the rest of the world, I had no way of knowing what the result was until I could 'wire myself back into the mainframe' when stopping to connect in Los Angeles. The temptation was too much to resist, and as soon as I was off the plane I was firing up the laptop and logging into the airport's wifi to put me out of my misery.

I was doing this while standing in the queue to go through security, and border guards rarely take a rosy view of a man fiddling about with a laptop in a mildly panicked state in an airport. Especially not American border guards. A girl was patrolling back and forth in the queue, and came up to me pretty quickly.

"Can you put your device away, please, sir?"

"Sure, no problem."

At this point I left the laptop on top of my suitcase, hoping that I could load up the result before she came back. That didn't happen.

"Sir, Please put your device away, it is not allowed at this time."

It still hadn't loaded.

"Please put your device away *now*, sir."

And it swiftly became apparent that my credit at the Bank of LA Border Guards was running low. As I started to flip the screen down, I saw the result flash up on the screen. It was not the news I wanted to read. But then, it was time to get checked through security and I had to stay in the good books of the man behind the desk. Trying to be polite and courteous is less than easy when you've a) just come off a 12-hour flight and b) have literally just found out your team has lost 3-1 and is out of the FA Cup. Then there was a minor misunderstanding when he stuck his thumb in the air, which I took for meaning 'OK – all done' and led to me reciprocating with the same gesture. He looked at me like I was a blithering idiot and said 'Put your thumb on the screen so I can take your prints.' Suitably reprimanded, I toddled off to the business lounge, to which a Danish lady with whom I'd struck up a conversation on the plane had invited me.

It was just as I sat down on a lovely comfy sofa that I looked up to see Robbie Williams' face. Once I realised that it wasn't the TV in front of me and it was actually him, I tried taking a photo of him. Word of advice – if you're going to try and pap a pop star, don't do it with the flash on. It tends to make said pop stars less than agreeable when you ask to have your photo taken with them 20 seconds later. I thought about trying to explain my cycling adventures, but it was pretty clear that Port Vale's most famous fan wasn't interested. Never mind – his loss!

I got back home on Sunday (February 17), with just five days to prepare for the mammoth two-day trek to Carlisle. One important aspect of the ride was that I would be riding in memory of Ian Cuff, a member of one of the Dons' disability teams who had recently passed away. Strangely, the idea of doing so was borne out of a slight mix-up earlier in the season. I'd been desperate for donations during the autumn and Dan (with his dark sense of humour) said he would donate £10 if I called the ride to Tranmere in November the 'Dan McCalla Memorial Ride'. The SET's Matt Cove thought Dan had actually died and was quite concerned initially, but when I assured him that he was still very much alive, Matt suggested that a real memorial ride would be an excellent idea.

I never got to meet Ian, but I'd heard a lot about him. He hadn't had the breaks in life and he was in a tough position physically due to his congenital heart disease. Matt explained to me that Ian had embodied the spirit of the SET teams through his passion and commitment right up until he died in 2012. When he passed away, his cortege passed stadium:mk with the rest of the SET players, several members of the first team and a number of the staff all forming a guard of honour for him, such was the esteem in which he was held within the organisation. He was never able to watch many first-team away games due to his disability, so we thought it fitting that I could carry his memory to Carlisle, that most 'hardcore' of away days that almost any Dons fan would want to do given the choice and the money to do so.

I was also kept extremely busy during that week leading up to Carlisle by the amount of admin work I was having to do around the project. A sponsor, Brooks Precision Engineering of Aylesbury, had donated £350 just for me to do the Carlisle ride. I was really happy to go and visit them, but without sounding ungrateful, small things like this were taking precious time out of what was (at least for me) a crucial week of the season.

The amount of media attention had heightened significantly as the longest ride of them all approached, too. I was using up a lot of energy having to 'push' the project to get it noticed, and that in the vast majority of cases it was me feeding the story to the journalists, rather than them making the effort to call me. Carl Sewell, a fellow Dons fan who works for PR firm SmashIt had been my one big help in that respect, getting me into *Shoot* magazine and *The League Paper*. But even with the two local papers in Milton Keynes, and to an extent with the communications from the club itself, it had been really tough to get much significant coverage.

It had all underlined to me the advantages of being a bigger cause and having large numbers of people willing to fly the flag for you and make the efforts to get that publicity. As merely one man, I was always going to be up against it, but the efforts that had been made on that front by other Dons fans in my name on that front was crucial in getting my story out to the wider public.

The biggest PR coup I managed was getting a piece on BBC *Look East* on the Friday of my ride to Carlisle. It came thanks to the sterling efforts of field reporter Jessica Cooper, who brought a camera down to film the start of my ride on the Friday morning. But even that took five months of planning. Jessica had been following and championing my story ever since I first made contact with her before the Bury game in mid-September. Eventually, only five seconds of the filming she did at stadium:mk was used, and the entire piece was only around 80 seconds in total, but to get the project onto regional prime-time TV made all that hard work worthwhile.

This publicity spike was matched by an extra bit of attention from the people who knew me ahead of the ride they rightly considered to be the most challenging and the least sane. I'd put the route up on Facebook before I left, and I'd had a battery of messages from my fellow members of Leighton Buzzard Road Cycling Club. There's a term in cycling used to describe hard riding called 'chapeau', and quite a few of the Facebook messages and texts I received simply said: 'chapeau, mate!' These messages were from hardened, seasoned long-distance cyclists: the kind of madmen that go to France every year to ride *Etape du Tour*, the huge public ride on a full mountain stage of the Tour de France a few days after the race itself has tackled it. That should have inspired some confidence in me, but if anything I felt more nervous. If these guys were bristling at such a long route, then what the hell was I up against?!

Five days back in the UK wouldn't have normally been a problem, but the 25 hours of flying time from Auckland had really taken their toll. I desperately wanted to get back out on the bike, but I just couldn't do it. I was just completely spent of energy by about 3pm every day, and I didn't really feel like something remotely resembling normal condition until the Thursday, the day before I left for Cumbria. That day I managed to get out and do 20 miles, which was as much as I could manage, but the icy wind that was sweeping across the Bedfordshire countryside around my home really wasn't helping matters.

At the time, I also felt the massive amount of riding I'd done while in New Zealand probably didn't do me much good. As well as the 152-mile Oldham substitute ride, I'd done another 60 miles during the week commuting back and forth to the office I was working from, and also did a monster 40-mile climbing session in the Waitakeres with a local cycling club. All this was in 25-degree heat and in very bright sunlight to boot. That proved I was fit enough to do the ride, but ultimately meant that I had to rest most of that week I was back in the UK.

One welcome distraction came on Wednesday night, when my friend Jules helped me give my bike a good service. And by 'service', I mean a complete strip-down and rebuild in his professional workshop: at 5:00pm we changed the wheels and cables, cleaned and polished everything, checked the brakes and then put it all together again. By 9:00 we were coming towards the end of what had been an incredibly long process, but Jules's infectious enthusiasm for the task hadn't dimmed. He was knelt on the floor finishing off the polish job, and he turned to me and said: "It's ready". I just wish I could have said the same about myself.

Thursday, the last day before the ride, was a blur. I remember waking up thinking that: "This time tomorrow, I'll be riding to Carlisle", and ten hours later, sitting down to dinner, I remember thinking "This time tomorrow, I'll STILL be riding to Carlisle, and I'll only be halfway there!". It was about midnight before I managed to get to sleep, and I just felt numb inside. I think my body was just frozen in pure expectation by then.

I woke early on the Friday morning, and started getting ready for The Big One. Well, if you really can call 'sitting at the table and barely being able to lift spoonfuls of porridge into my mouth' preparations. I was just sat staring into the distance in my kitchen, wishing that Carlisle could have come just one week later. Margaret agreed that it had all come too soon, but she also correctly pointed out that there was no point sugarcoating things. The fixture computer set Carlisle United vs Milton Keynes Dons as Saturday February 23. I had no choice in the matter and I just had to get on with it. But looking back, there's no doubt in my mind that I started the Carlisle ride in worse shape physically than any other ride all season.

Riding from home up to the stadium for the 'official' start early that morning, I started to feel nervous as it dawned on me just what I was doing. I almost felt like a pro cyclist, riding through the 'neutral zone' at a steady pace before the real stage got underway. About three miles into the nine-mile roll to the stadium, I felt a little thirsty, and reached down for a water bottle. All I felt was empty metal bottle-holder. Then I looked down and realised that in my mental numbness, I, Adam Faiers, being of sound body and organised mind, had left both my water bottles at home for the biggest ride of the season and possibly my life. To quote my personal mentor Edmund Blackadder: "Bugger".

I'd spent all that time getting myself as prepared as possible, only to leave the two bottles of water sitting on the sideboard in my kitchen. I was practically beside myself with rage at my own incompetence. I phoned Chris, who would be driving a 'support car' to accompany me from Rockingham Castle in Corby onwards, and he said he'd bring extra ones for me. But that still meant I had to cover the first 50 miles without any liquid sustenance whatsoever – hardly ideal. So I guzzled whatever I could get hold of at the stadium to stock my fluids up. I remain forever indebted to Anne, the ever-cheery Dons receptionist, for that cup of coffee she made me that morning.

Jessica was coming to film the start at the stadium for *Look East*, but as anyone who's worked in TV will know, that's rarely a swift process. I met her at the stadium at 8:15am and did a phone interview for BBC Three Counties Radio, but was then informed that her cameraman was running late. That pushed my schedule back, and I quickly realised that I would miss my planned 9:00 departure time – irritating, but a worthy sacrifice for the publicity.

The cameraman arrived at 8:30 and promptly began his filming. Which went on. And on. And on, until I suddenly looked at my watch and realised it was 9:45, and he still hadn't finished. That wouldn't have bothered me, but it was a particularly cold morning and a biting icy wind was sweeping around the stadium:mk car park. By 9:45 my legs had very much gone right through the shivering phase, out the other side and firmly lodged themselves into the realm of an uncontrollable juddering.

While all this was going on, a crowd was gathering around us, mainly Dons and SET staff that emerged from their lovely warm offices into the Arctic cold of Milton Keynes to wave me off. Among them was a lady I'd never met before, who helped warm my cockles a little by thanking me for all the help my work was doing for her son, who was part of the SET squad. I'd often thought about all the equipment that my raised funds was buying, but that was the first time I'd really got a chance to stop and think about the tangible benefits to the people who were actually using them. I like to think that gave me a bit of perspective about the whole thing that perhaps I was missing previously.

Then Karl Robinson pulled up in his car and came over for a quick chat. He gave me the standard words to say thanks for my efforts and so on, but then I turned to him and blurted out the thoughts in my head for no apparent reason.

"If the team perform, we can still get in the play-offs, Karl. Can we do it?"

At any other time, I'm sure Karl would have been glad to talk about the team's prospects, which weren't great at the time as we were 12 points off the play-off spots with only 16 league games left to play. Unfortunately, it came at the precise moment that the cameraman decided to raise his all-seeing lens and point it squarely in our direction.

"You would ask me that question when there's a bloody camera on us, wouldn't you?" Karl said playfully. I felt bad about it, but he took it in his stride and firmly shook my hand.

Then, as the icing on the cake for my departure, Pete Winkelman came down from the chairman's office. He stood right next to me, looked at me and simply asked how it was going.

"It's going great," I replied. "We've managed to raise almost £3000 so far."

On that remark, he grabbed my gaze, and I don't know if it was just the normal infectious Winkelman enthusiasm, but all he could do was gasp.

"£3000?! That's an incredible amount for one person to raise!"

If Pete thought that that was impressive, then I definitely must be doing something right. He asked me about the route I was taking and his eyebrows lifted as I said I was trying to reach Ilkley by the end of the day.

"I'm going to Ilkley because I want to go through the Dales to Hawes," I explained.

STADIUM CHASE

"Hawes, really? Blimey," he replied. He obviously knew the area, and I didn't think he sounded particularly hopeful about my chances.

Finally, two hours after reaching the stadium, I pushed off to great applause at 10:00am. There was a three-two-one and off I went, out of the stadium car park and onto the MK grid roads, north towards the town centre. This was actually it now. Milton Keynes to Carlisle. By bike. Really.

That horrible wind that had frozen my calves was blowing from the east, which was more bad news as I had to initially head east to get to Olney before riding north towards Wellingborough and Corby. I kept going north, through the centre of MK, but I just couldn't bring myself to turn right and face that wind head-on until the absolute last moment. After about three miles against it, I reached junction 14 of the M1 and the Milton Keynes Coachway, the terminal for National Express coaches calling from all over the country. Having spent two hours getting really cold at the stadium while all the filming was going on, I just had to stop for a bit to warm myself up before I really did myself some damage. Thank God I didn't see a coach with 'Carlisle' advertised as a destination. I probably would have jumped on it there and then and left my bike chained to the railings.

My mouth was so cold that I couldn't close it properly and there were bits of dribble coming out that I couldn't stop – not my most auspicious moment of my season, it has to be said. My legs still felt like two giant blocks of ice, too. When I got into the Coachway, I rang Chris to let him know that I'd be late meeting him at Rockingham, and once I rang off I realised that I needed the toilet. But using the loos cost 30p and I had no change.

I went to the information desk and tried to appeal to the better nature of the bod behind the counter, but he simply shrugged. He didn't care. For all he knew I was only riding another 400 yards, not 260 miles, so I didn't blame him for brushing me off. Still didn't help though!

After another ten minutes in the warmth of the terminal, I plucked up the courage to get back on the bike. As I did so, a man came up to me and said:

"Oh, you're the guy who's doing all these bike rides for the Dons!"

"Yeah, that's me. I'm just on my way to Carlisle now."

As soon as that C-word left my lips, I realise how absurd that sounded to a man who was probably hopping on a coach to Luton Airport or something. He wished me luck. I should have asked him for 30p to use the gents. I regretted not doing so for most of the morning.

Back on the road, I passed Newport Pagnell on the A509 and found myself warming up and getting into a rhythm, lifting my spirits hugely. The film crew had relocated to Olney high street, a few miles further on, and waved me by as they got an 'action' shot for Jessica's report. That was another big lift given the long day ahead, which was somewhat strange given that that very film crew was the reason I was running so late in the first place.

I set my mind to the task at hand and managed to get through Wellingborough, Kettering and up towards Corby without any problems. In fact, I was doing a pretty good job of keeping up with the film crew. On the approach to Rockingham Castle, there was a drop downhill towards where Chris said he'd meet me (as would the film crew, who would get one last shot of me, presumably before I crossed the *Look East* televisual border into *East Midlands Today* bandit country). I thought that'd be a great chance to come sweeping down at 40mph, tucked up on the handlebars for the telly, doing my best impression of Chris Froome descending an Alp.

Those plans were dashed by one minor thing. For health and safety reasons, the film crew had to wear hi-vis jackets. And if you're a motorist and you see a man in a hi-vis jacket at the side of the road pointing a camera at you, what do you think it's going to be? Struck by complete paranoid fear of the speed camera patrol that wasn't a speed camera patrol, all the cars around me nailed themselves to 30mph all the way down the hill. That left me, the cyclist, stuck behind them and ruined my chance at making my own bit of TV gold!

At Rockingham, I did another quick interview for Jessica before she said goodbye, and I then took the opportunity for ten minutes of heated rest inside Chris's car and a much-needed drink. Then we set off again towards Oakham and then Newark, sticking mainly to quieter country roads so that Chris would be able to follow me without causing almighty traffic jams behind.

As I approached Newark, I was feeling much more confident, having got through such a difficult early section. I was motoring along at a good 18mph, I was fully warmed up and I was feeling pretty bullish about the challenge ahead of me, which was to get to Ilkley and then decamp to the Holiday Inn in Leeds, my overnight stopping point before I tried to haul my carcass over the Yorkshire Dales on Saturday morning. To many of those I knew, my choice of route, running roughly parallel with the A1 to Leeds and then cutting over the Dales seemed odd, especially as the natural way to travel north to Carlisle by road is to head to the west of the Pennines rather than east.

But there was method in my madness; the Holiday Inn in Leeds had kindly agreed to sponsor me by providing room and board overnight, and there was also the crucial factor that (believe it or not) going that way was less hilly than trying to go over the Peak District. The actual distance of the Leeds route was a few miles longer, but there was no doubt in my mind that the amount of energy I'd need to expend would be smaller. Then again, one way or another I was going to have to tackle the Lake District and there was no way of dodging that bullet.

By this point in the season, I'd got to know the Leeds route quite well, because it had become my standard route of choice for many of the games that we'd played up north. It was comforting to know that a big chunk of the Carlisle ride would be spent on roads that I already knew and felt relatively at home on. Newark held some raw memories for me because of the flood I'd had to deal with en route to Doncaster in December, but this time it was perfectly dry. I flew straight through, but soon after that, at around the 90-mile mark, the day finally started to catch up with me. It was 3:30pm by this point, so I'd been riding for five and a half hours on and off, and I was starting to feel very hungry, very thirsty (a consequence of the self-inflicted lack of fluids at the start of the day) and was suffering in the energy stakes.

It was at this point that having Chris with me was the critical factor in keeping going. I managed to reach the 100-mile mark and stopped at the trusty McDonald's at Markham Moor and promptly got myself some food. But just as I sat down with my tray, I began to shiver uncontrollably, for the second time that day. I tried to think past it, but 20 minutes later I'd finished my food and I was still shivering just as much.

Chris put his coat around me, took me out of McDonald's and bundled me into his car. It took me over an hour to warm up to a body temperature I would consider being anywhere close to acceptable. To this day, I still have no idea what I would have done if I hadn't had him with me and I'd been stuck shivering in a McDonald's 100 miles from home on my own.

It was 6:00pm by the time I was ready to go again, and therefore dark, which brings its own set of advantages and challenges. As much as I still had to deal with the wind, as a hardy long-distance athlete of many years I've always found that the temperature rises a little just after nightfall. At that time of day, everything magically seems to calm down a little and you feel a bit of quietness and peace around you compared to the hustle and bustle of the day.

In the gathering darkness, I got up to and through Doncaster, passing the scene of my mascot race debut at the Racecourse, as well as the Keepmoat Stadium (where, for the second time this season, I arrived without there being any football to watch!), and from then on I was in unknown territory for the last section of day one up to Leeds. By this point, it was obvious that I wasn't going to reach Ilkley until the following day. There's quite a bit of climbing over the moors before you drop down into Leeds, and although I made decent going to start with, I slowed right down to the point where it took me three and a half exhausting hours to cover the last 50 miles into the city itself.

That made it 9:30pm by the time I reached the Holiday Inn, some 11 and a half hours since I'd left Milton Keynes. Relief washed through my body. I'd been out in a biting headwind since 7:45 that morning and cycled 150 miles in the process. Thoughts raced through my head at all the basic mundane things I could do. 'I can sleep! I can drink! I can wash!'

Strangely, I didn't really want to eat very much, and I actually began to feel sick shortly after I stopped. I'd eaten a couple of snacks on the way in, and I'd had my McDonald's, but when I arrived in the hotel restaurant and was presented with the menu options by the waitress, a switch suddenly clicked inside my brain. A switch marked 'EAT FOOD NOW'.

"Do you want lasagne, love?"
"Yes!"
"Do you want garlic bread?"
"Yes!"
"Do you want chips?"
"Yes! Yes! Yes!"

The girl, Rachel, knew who I was and why I was staying there, so my willingness to indulge in a calorie intake Andy Murray would have been proud of came as no surprise to her. Chris had phoned the hotel to let them know I was late, and Rachel very kindly waited so that she could help me when I arrived. After I ordered the food, she told me to go and get showered and promised to have my dinner ready when I returned to the restaurant. As I was greeted with the aforementioned feast, she insisted on buying me a drink.

"What'll it be, then?"

"I really don't think I can cope with much. Just a mineral water would be lovely, thanks."

"Look, I'm buying you a drink!" she said, in her heavy Leeds accent. "Now, what do you want?"

"Fine, whisky it is then!"

It took me an hour to eat that dinner, partly due to my body trying to rest and partly because there was so much of it. By the time I got into bed it was 11:45 and, unsurprisingly, I was asleep as soon as my head hit the pillow.

That deep sleep lasted all of one hour, as I was gradually aroused from my slumber by the throbbing aches that were coming from my feet and from my knees. Getting back to sleep was then made virtually impossible by the racket made by drunken Yorkshiremen and Yorkshirewomen coming back to their hotel rooms from their nights out – such is life staying in a city centre hotel on a Friday night. The room next to mine was populated by a couple having the most blazing of rows, with the woman ceaselessly shouting: "You're a bum! You're a bum!" at her partner. I've no idea what he'd done to deserve such treatment, but it was obviously something pretty serious. Perhaps he was a Leeds fan that had promised to cycle to Plymouth Argyle for charity. I mean, who would be stupid enough to do something like that…?

Deprived of any sleep, I decided to get out of bed and stretch out my aching limbs and joints. All I could think of then was the fact that I had to be up at 4:30am to get out at 5:30 to give myself enough time to reach Carlisle. My visit to the Leeds Holiday Inn was very much a flying one! As the first leg had taken so long that we never made it to Ilkley, where we'd intended to stop, drive to the hotel, and then return to for a restart, so we had to start Saturday's journey extra-early to make up for the 20 miles we'd 'given away' the previous day.

I managed to get a bit more sleep before dragging myself out of bed at 4:30. The manageress on duty, Zoe, sorted me out some breakfast that consisted of enough coffee and croissants to sink a French galleon. Come 5:30 I started heading out through Leeds, passing gang after gang of inebriated blokes staggering home from what had clearly been heavy nights on the tiles. At least they were nice drunks rather than angry drunks: at one point I signalled to go right at a roundabout, and a group of them to my right started to cheer because they thought I was waving at them!

The roads out of Leeds were huge wide expanses with bus lanes, which put me at ease a little, but very soon they started to climb. And not just little climbs, but proper intense gradients. These carried on all the way to Ilkley (there's no way I would have managed to get that far on the Friday night, had I attempted to do so), where I stopped at 6:30 to do another phone interview for BBC Three Counties Radio that they would carry through their Saturday morning news bulletins. As I continued past Skipton and towards the village of Gargrave, I remembered doing canoe races from Leeds to Liverpool on the canal system about 20 years previously. That formed my next mental target, because I knew that Gargrave would bring an end to this section of climbing.

Normally, I would therefore have been elated to reach Gargrave. And I would have been if it wasn't for the fact that it had started to snow. The next 27 miles along the A65, past Settle and Giggleswick and along as far as Kirkby Lonsdale, was a long section that just did not seem to end. It went up and up, there were loads of heavy lorries on the road, and I felt so tired.

I had stopped at Settle (a rather apt location given the snowfall) when Chris and I debated where we would take our next stop. I was 35 miles into the second leg by this point, so I thought I could manage the next 20 to Kirkby Lonsdale and we could regroup there before making the decisive turn north towards the Lake District. I carried on, but it wasn't long before I felt completely out of energy.

I was now at around the 200-mile mark overall, making this the longest ride I'd ever done even at that point, and I was beginning to feel things that I'd just never felt before. The extreme tiredness and the pain in my shoulders was excruciating, so reaching Kirkby Lonsdale was a huge mental lift. With just 54 miles to go to reach Carlisle, I was convinced that it had to be pretty much all downhill from then on, having spent a long gruelling morning of climbing barely without respite. After a cup of coffee and a bacon roll, I logged onto Twitter and happily proclaimed that I had just 54 miles to go and that I'd really broken the back of the ride. How wrong could I have been?

It took about two minutes of riding out of Kirkby Lonsdale for my worst fears to be confirmed. The road north just kept climbing; up it went, getting steeper and steeper as I carried on. I saw some cyclists coming the other way (i.e. down) and they were firing down the hill at some ridiculous speed. Lucky gits. At least they didn't have to deal with constant steep climbs and ever-increasing snowfall.

There was a short link road that carried me over to the A6, the main road that would carry me all the way to Carlisle. When I saw it on the map, I'd assumed that it looked so short because it was exceptionally steep, and I was proved absolutely right. Plugging away on the pedals, within a few minutes I looked around and suddenly realised that everything around me had gone white. I'd ascended above the snow line.

It was one of those rides where you will yourself on by thinking: "It'll all drop downhill just round that next corner". And then when it doesn't, you keep going to the next one and hope it drops there. But that moment never seemed to come, and I kept climbing. I'd managed to convince myself that I was on the wrong road, on the basis that it really should have started to drop by now. There was no chance of that really happening, of course, as my GPS was pre-programmed to keep me on the right road and Chris would have alerted me if I'd strayed off-course, but when you're as tired as I was at the time, the mind wanders.

Up... and up... and up I went. I started to think of all my heroes from watching pro cycling through the years, thinking: "This hill is just a training ride for them. Man up and keep going." I passed this incredible viaduct that reminded me of the train line to Hogwarts, and then I passed underneath the M6. As I emerged from the underpass, all I could see was white everywhere, apart from the black ribbon of road stretching outwards and upwards directly in front of me. I was standing up on the pedals by this stage, pumping away for dear life, because I truly felt that if I stopped at any point, I wouldn't have it within my body to get going again. Looking back, all that climbing over the Waitakeres probably helped me there. I remembered the constant mashing of gears up those mountains, and it replaced my general sense of despair with a resilience to get on with the bloody thing.

Then there was a helpful plateau and a lay-by where Chris, who had been driving ahead of me, had pulled in. I pulled up beside him and muttered something like: "This is suffering, isn't it?" He nodded in sympathetic return. I was still 39 miles away and was worried that I might not get to Brunton Park in time for kick-off, but then it occurred to me that with three inches of snow covering the area, the game was probably going to be called off. Little did I know at the time that not a single flake of snow had descended anywhere near Carlisle!

As I started again, the road mercifully turned downwards and started snaking around the M6. I got about three miles of downhill, which felt like heaven. It was like falling off a cliff, but on a bike. And obviously it wouldn't hurt so much when I reached the bottom. It was incredible to fly through these snow-covered valleys, in and out of hills, feeling like I was racing the traffic on the motorway. But then the road started climbing yet again towards Tebay and the Shap Summit, and the icy wind was starting to make any movement whatsoever a real challenge.

The snow was falling so heavily that it was starting to accumulate not just on the fields or the road, but on my person. Layers of the white stuff started to coat my helmet and my back. It was when I stopped at one set of traffic lights and a clump of snow fell off my helmet, passed my face and hit the floor under my pedals that I realised I was in a spot of bother. I pulled in shortly afterwards, and told Chris that this was taking things too far. I was raising the white flag.

"This is just ridiculous, mate," I said. "I'm not managing much more than 10mph in this weather and I think we should just stop and drive to some lower ground. No-one is going to think any less of me for stopping because of this, and quite frankly, I don't really care if they do or not right now. We just need to get off this high ground."

I put the bike onto Chris's roof rack, I slumped into the passenger seat, and he pulled out and drove away.

Yep, that's right. You can go back and read that last bit again if you need some time to deal with the shock of that statement. I did not manage to cycle all the way to Carlisle. I cheated. I got a lift for a bit of it. And given the conditions, I'm not in the least bit ashamed to admit it.

Chris knew the area pretty well, and drove me down to the village of Shap, which was about six miles further on from where I'd stopped. In those six miles we dropped from around 1100 feet above sea level to around 700 feet, bringing us back down below the snow line. While in the car, I tweeted my surrender: "After a tactical decision to get out of the blizzard, I've driven about 6miles off the high ground to Shap. Figured I wanted to stay alive!"

The responses I had to that were mercifully positive, as people fully understood that my safety was more important than being able to say: "I did it". But the next problem was that I was going to have to get back on the bike at some point. Chris couldn't just drive me all the way from Shap to Carlisle (as much of a relief as that would have been). For the last couple of miles before I left the car, all I could think was: "I don't want to do this". And the icy wind that greeted me as I left the car and put the bike back on the road just added to the negativity brewing inside my aching, screaming muscles.

Then my mind went all Winston Churchill on me and gave my body a stern talking to. It went something like this:

"There's a point that everyone faces in life where you have to do something you don't want to do. It could be a job interview, a work meeting, or whatever, where every bone in your body is yelling 'don't do it'. You've got to get on with this."

And so it was thanks to that mental oration that I clambered back onto the bike in Shap and began to tackle the 28 miles that still stood between me and Brunton Park. And from there on in, it was pretty straightforward: still long and tiring, but an absolute doddle compared to what I'd already faced. Although it didn't feel like it, it was more or less downhill all the way from that point, and those last few miles really couldn't come quickly enough.

I'd tweeted earlier that I thought I was going to arrive at the ground at 2:30pm, just half an hour before kick-off, but I was struggling to even keep to that target and it was beginning to look tighter and tighter time-wise as I desperately tried to make it there before 3:00. As I reached the outskirts of Carlisle, the traffic began to build up again and it gave me a bizarre sense of companionship, as if I wasn't riding completely alone through a desolate landscape. I was trying to push on along with the traffic, and if anything it told my mind to make the legs go faster. I felt as if I was riding quicker as I soldiered on towards the city centre.

I stopped at some traffic lights and asked the guy in the car alongside me which way was the quickest to the football ground. I had a pretty good idea of it, and I had it programmed into the GPS, but in my slightly delirious state those facts simply failed to register. He told me to turn left and keep going straight to reach the ground. Great, I thought, the last bit… until I rounded the corner and was greeted with a residential road so cobbled that you could have told gullible tourists it was Coronation Street and relieved them of £5 notes.

It wasn't very long, but the cobbles and the speed humps jarred through my joints and really narked me. But eventually I caught sight of the Brunton Park floodlights that signalled journey's end. I was hoping to come in down the middle of the road, arms aloft as if I'd won the Tour de France, but the traffic was far too busy for that. So I pulled up outside the club shop at 2:40 to find Margaret and about 20 Dons fans waiting for my arrival… by looking the other way, further down the road. It turns out they were all expecting me to come from the other direction, and I would have got away with the surprise entrance of the century had Dan not turned around, clocked me about ten metres away and screamed "YEAHHH!".

I'd made it (well, sort of, as I had hitched a ride for a bit of it). It was such a relief to see my wife and all of my friends who'd travelled up for the match by coach, car or train that morning, and that was what really made it sink in. These were the people who had supported my project financially, and had sent me countless good luck messages for all the rides that I'd done. The small band of people that sit and stand with me week-in, week-out at every away game the Dons play, all over the country. They were here.

STADIUM CHASE

I was here. Thank God for that!

I'd tried to contact Carlisle United in advance to see if they had any facilities I could use but I never got a response from them. In the heavy traffic, I'd got split up from Chris and hence all my change of clothes and stood outside the ground. In the end, I thought it would be warmer to wait inside, plus I was missing the game, so at about 3:15, with the match well underway, I entered the away stand. The moment my head appeared above the parapet, my senses were assaulted by the ungodly scream that Dan charitably calls his singing voice reverberating from the back of the stand.

"He bikes for the Dons, he bikes for the Do-o-o-ons, Adam Faiers, HE BIKES FOR THE DONS!"

Within moments, most of the other 180 fans that had made the trip up had joined in, too. And that just felt so fantastic. If there was anything to cement the magnitude of what I'd just done in my own head, that was it.

I was carrying my helmet and gave it to Margaret to look after, as I then saw Chris, who had come into the ground to find me. As my stuff was still in the car, we needed to go out again so we walked down to ask a steward to temporarily let us out. Normally, once you leave, you are aren't allowed to re-enter, but we hoped they would understand that this was a special case.

As I approached the Chief Steward, he said to me: "Sir, I respect the fact that you want to cycle to the game and you've brought your helmet into the ground. But are you sure the people you've given it to are going to treat your property with the same respect as you would?"

"I've only given it to my wife! I think it'll be OK! Besides, I've just cycled all the way here from Milton Keynes and these people all know me, so I don't think it'll be a problem."

Cue a long pause from the steward, before he spluttered:

"...you've what?"

"I said I've just cycled here from Milton Keynes."

Cue another long pause.

"No, you haven't, mate"

"Yes, I have," I replied, at which point I revealed my MK Dons cycling jersey, which amongst other layers I was still wearing."

Cue a third long pause and a second quizzical look.

"Bloody hell. Well done, mate." We made a lot of friends with the stewards that day.

It seems slightly silly to have gone all that way by bike to watch a football match, and to have pushed so hard to make it there in time for kick-off, and to then barely remember a thing about the match itself. My vague recollections of the game include Adam Chicksen's first-ever league goal that deservedly put us 1-0 up at half-time. But we struggled in the second half, and with 'keeper David Martin taken off with an injury just before the interval, it was taking a little while for second-choice goalie Ian McLoughlin to get up to speed. The Dons failed to clear the ball from a Carlisle corner five minutes from the end, and the Cumbrians managed to pinch an equaliser. It finished 1-1, which extended our winless run in the league to six games. But at the time I felt too tired and numb to feel aggrieved about it.

The one thing I can remember vividly was some Carlisle fan on the other side of the divide between home and away fans giving us a load of V-signs when the equaliser went in, but more surprisingly, that huge numbers of Carlisle fans were walking past him to go home as he did so. I just couldn't understand why fans would leave a game five minutes before the end when their team has just levelled things up. Maybe it was because they didn't feel a necessity to stay to the end and get their money's worth as they hadn't travelled 260 miles to get to the game, but even now I still think it was daft for them to desert the ground just as their team was pushing forwards for the win.

STADIUM CHASE

Coming out of the ground at full-time, all the other Dons fans were giving me congratulations and patting me on the back and so on. Even their stewards all gave me a round of applause, which was an especially nice touch. Very quickly I was back in the car with Chris and speeding down the M6 to get home, and I actually began to feel slightly intimidated about what I'd just done. We stopped at Tebay services an hour into the drive, and I gazed out at the snow-covered hills. "I've just been up them," I thought to myself. "I can't truly believe I've just been up that." If you'd showed me those hills early that morning, driven me down to Leeds and then told me to get on my bike and ride over them to Carlisle, I genuinely wouldn't have believed I could have done it.

I was listening to BBC Five Live's football phone-in *606* in the car, when my mind clicked back into action as the presenter, Mark Chapman, said: "Send us a text, let us know what you've been up to today." So, completely on a whim, I sent a text to the number given explaining my ride, and within a minute the show's producer had phoned me straight back.

"I just want to check – is this actually true?" he asked accusingly, as if it was all a massive wind-up.

"Absolutely," I replied. "Have a look at the MKDSA website if you don't believe me."

He hung up, and obviously went straight onto the MKDSA page, where a couple of news stories detailing my progress had been put up. A couple of minutes later, he rang me back.

"Right, we're going to put you straight on with Mark and Robbie [Savage]."

Five minutes after that, I hung up after completing a spur-of-the-moment national radio interview that couldn't have gone much better if I'd spent three months rehearsing for it. Mark and Robbie were both on good form and seemed genuinely appreciative of my efforts, especially when Mark more or less demanded that I publicised my JustGiving website.

Shortly after the interview, I fell asleep in the car for an hour or so, and when I woke up, I saw that my phone was flashing with some crazy number of emails in my inbox. I noticed they were all JustGiving notifications, which I thought was very strange. I fired up my browser, opened my JustGiving page and was given a real shock.

In the time I'd been asleep, more than a dozen football fans from clubs all over the country had put their hands in their pockets and donated to my project. I just couldn't believe the response I'd got from people who had never heard of me until I'd got myself onto *606*. Some of the messages they'd left alongside their donations were simply heart-warming:

"Heard you on *606*. Great cause, awesome challenge. Best of luck for the rest of this season's away games. Ipswich fan."

"What an awesome thing to do! Best of luck to MK Dons from a Seattle Sounders FC supporter in the USA."

"Millwall calling. Well done fella, truly inspiring."

"Superb effort. Best of luck for the rest of the season from a Leeds fan. Marching (or should that be cycling?) on together!"

"Heard you on 5Live. I am a Portsmouth season ticket holder and will be at the game [against the Dons] on Tuesday. Safe journey to Fratton Park. Play up Pompey."

"Heard you on Radio 5. Top effort, and I don't even like football..."

Fans of countless other teams had donated, too: Derby, Manchester United, Notts County, Middlesbrough,

STADIUM CHASE

Chelsea and Newcastle were all represented, and they were just the ones who mentioned which teams they supported. All in all, I raised another £400 from those fans, and *606*-generated donations kept on coming in for another week or so after that.

Despite all the emotions of the previous two days, it was reading those comments that brought me to tears, more or less for the only time all season. I'd never expected such a reaction from the wider football community, mainly because many people still don't like MK Dons because of the way the team came into existence in Milton Keynes. To me it proved that to some people, the MK Dons are a normal team with normal supporters, in many ways just like every other club, and that ultimately we as football fans are all in this together. The fact that my total raised had jumped from £3000 to £3700 over the course of the two days was simply the icing on the cake.

But not everything was rosy. My feet were in a dreadful state, and my right heel was bleeding after some road salt worked itself inside my shoe earlier that morning – literally rubbing salt into the wound. My left foot was also sore and had swollen to the point that it was extremely uncomfortable to keep it in my shoe.

What I needed most was plenty of time for recovery, but I knew that I was little more than 48 hours away from having to cycle another 120 miles to Portsmouth on Tuesday. I kept thinking: "In one hour, I need to be better than I am now, and in two hours, better than that." It was going to be a difficult few days. I wish I could have savoured the achievement of cracking Carlisle fully. But the fixture list didn't lie. Fratton Park was calling...

CHAPTER 8: THE NEVER-ENDING WINTER

I slept most of the two days between Carlisle and Portsmouth, even though I was technically awake most of the time. I was floating around, practically in a daze, going through my usual post-ride and pre-ride routines without consciously thinking about them. I had to clean my kit and my bike, as well as checking my computer to watch yet more donations flood in. The Carlisle adventure, and the publicity surrounding it, had pushed my total towards the £4000 mark, and I fully believed that I could reach £5000 by the end of the season, with seven rides to go and some sidelines planned that would hopefully bring in even more cash.

I was fairly relaxed about the 110-mile ride down to Portsmouth once it came around on the Tuesday (February 26), as Margaret's family hails from that part of the world and I knew the route down there pretty well. From Milton Keynes, it was down through Buckinghamshire to Chesham, then travelling around the outside of the western side of the M25, through Windsor and Ascot, down to Aldershot and Alton and then through rural Hampshire. The only real sting in the tail was going over the South Downs towards the end of the ride, but I'd planned to stop and visit some relatives in Alton and fill up with a nice cup of tea before tackling the hilliest part of the route.

I felt strange as I rode up to the stadium for the start on the Tuesday morning. It was almost an anticlimax in many ways, because everything over the previous few weeks (and in some ways, months) had been building up to Carlisle, and now that I'd done it, it felt like a bit of a comedown. I had a nice relaxed cup of coffee with my friend Dennis Woolford from the SET before I left, and by the time I saddled up and departed, it was noon. It was still a cold day, but there wasn't anything that was causing me any worries. That, my brief stop to visit my parents, and a call as I passed Aldermaston to be interviewed by one of the MK local papers meant I was a bit behind, and with it starting to get dark, I was a little concerned that my elderly relatives might start to get panicky about my whereabouts.

As I came into north Hampshire, there was a sizeable hill not far from Liss that I intended to attack, because it would act as a good barometer of how well I'd recovered from the exertions of Carlisle. My Garmin was able to log my whereabouts along the route at specific times, and when I got home from each ride, I was able to upload this data to Strava and compare my times for certain sections against those of other GPS users.

I'd been doing this for all the rides I'd carried the Garmin for, and my own personal Strava diary was littered with top ten times for short climbs and sprints all over the country, along with a couple of fastest times to boot. I knew that if I could get into the top ten on this Hampshire climb, then Carlisle had not caused any negative effects to my health. I managed a top ten time (comfortably, as it happened), and as I came onto the descent, I toggled through the modes on the Garmin to check my average speed for the ride to date. 24mph flashed back at me.

I thought to myself: "Woah, Adam, slow down! You don't need to be going this fast!" But I didn't feel like I was pushing myself to any particular extremes. Having been used to averages between 18 and 20mph for the longer rides I'd done, 24mph was in another league altogether. I deduced that Carlisle, and the preceding trip to New Zealand, hadn't damaged me at all – quite the opposite. The intensive long distances I'd covered, in both hot and cold conditions, had given me a huge step up in performance.

That speed allayed my relatives' fears, and after a lovely spot of tea, I completed the last leg to Portsmouth with a joyous descent all the way down to the coast, arriving at Fratton Park in plenty of time for the game. It was incredible to think that at the start of the season six months previously, I'd never attempted a 100-mile bike ride in my life. Now here I was batting them off like mere hors d'oeuvres. It sent me a powerful message of how much I had grown and was still growing as an athlete.

I turned into the terraced road that runs behind the main stand of Fratton Park, waving a quick hello to the Dons fans that had just piled off the coach cheering my arrival, and swung around to the right and the main entrance of the stadium. With its almost mock-Tudor facade, that entrance to Fratton Park is a real throwback to football of yesteryear, although I couldn't help but liken it to Harry Redknapp sitting in his Range Rover outside it giving quotes to massed reporters, back in the days before Pompey's astonishing fall from grace.

While a few more of our fans came up to me to offer their congratulations, what took me aback was that they were heavily outnumbered by the dozens of Portsmouth fans who came over to do the same. Many of them had heard me on *606* the previous Saturday, and so immediately recognised that a bloke in an MK Dons cycling top pulling up outside Fratton Park was going to be me, with quite a few placing cash into my hand to add to my fund. I'd had plenty of hospitable receptions from fans and club staff on my travels throughout the season, but the fact that this had an impromptu element to it was an extra touch that I really appreciated. I was then ushered inside the club offices, where I was given a private toilet on the third floor in which to get changed.

As Margaret's family are all big Portsmouth fans, I sympathised with the plight of the club, who at that time remained in administration and were the subject of a tug-of-war between the former owner and the supporters' trust that threatened the very existence of the club. It was a time when it was hard to see a way out and hard to see a sustainable future for Portsmouth FC, and yet despite that, around 10,000 fans still turned up every week. Portsmouth had started the season reasonably well, but from October they'd failed to win a game in nearly five months as the lack of cash meant their threadbare squad of players changed frequently. Even without the ten-point penalty lingering over them for going into administration, they were doomed to their third relegation in four seasons.

But still the fans came. They clearly weren't giving up, and I admired them a great deal for that. The amount of noise that the fans generated from the Fratton End that night was impressive, too – one of the best atmospheres I experienced at an away ground all season, and a welcome change given the sometimes sterile ambience at many clubs these days (my own included). The game finished 1-1, Portsmouth coming within inches of getting the win they had gone so long without by that point, while the Dons' awful away form continued as the side continued its slide towards mid-table obscurity.

As I got home and February turned into March, I was keen to try and find more ways to attract funds and publicity, and with only one ride in the first half of March thanks to a busy run of home games, I'd decided to try my hand at organising a celebrity darts night. The Dons had organised one at stadium:mk just before Christmas, which had proved incredibly popular, and I thought I'd be able to do something similar on a smaller scale that could generate a nice little profit for my fund.

This side-project, which I'd scheduled for March 16, following a home game against Tranmere, took up vastly more time in organisation than I'd bargained for, and it quickly turned into a nightmare. I'd found a suitable venue, Newport Pagnell Working Men's Club, and lined up three darts celebrities: 1983 world champion Keith Deller, Wayne 'Hawaii 501' Mardle and star announcer Russ Bray. It all sounded great, and at £12.50 a ticket including a fish and chip supper, I thought it was an absolute bargain. But the problems started when it came to selling tickets.

The darts personalities, of course, commanded fees for their appearances, and the cost of the food and venue hire meant I needed to sell just over 100 tickets to break even. I therefore had to sell a few more on top of that to make the profit that was the whole objective of the event. But people just didn't want to know. Everything that I tried, Facebook, Twitter, the MKDSA website, phoning round people, going around the bars at home games, just didn't work.

I'd sold about 20 tickets, a very long way short of what I actually needed, and I tried to hang on for as long as possible. I spoke to the likes of Russ to find out what the minimum fee was that I could get them to come down for, given that it was for charity. Russ was as helpful as he could be, but ultimately he had his own expenses to cover, and one week beforehand, I had to tell him that I was going to have to cancel, because based on ticket sales I was going to make a £1000 loss. Bearing in mind the money I'd been raising was intended for good causes, it just wasn't my money to gamble on a late rush of ticket sales. I was bitterly disappointed that I'd come so far short of making it happen, and it was the real low point of the whole season, even though it didn't involve a single metre of cycling.

What the whole debacle did teach me, though, was just how hard it is to market and sell things to football supporters. It gave me a huge amount of appreciation for just how hard a job the likes of club commercial director Andy Cullen and press officer Simone Corgan have to do to get Dons fans to part with their cash. Yes, the Dons' darts night was a success, but the club had to pull out all the stops with a marketing team able to go around selling tables to local businesses and the like. I, meanwhile, was merely one man trying to do the same in his spare time. I thought about it more over the summer during the planning of this book, and despite all the publicity efforts I'd made over the course of the season, I estimated that by the end of the season only about half of the Dons' 5700 season-ticket holders had ever heard of me, let alone endeavoured to find out more about the project. I'd assumed it was a lot more at the time.

I tried to put all that to the back of my mind and concentrated on the six remaining rides I still had to conquer. The first of those, on a freezing cold and horribly wet Saturday (March 9), was my second trip of the season to Sheffield. But this time, instead of heading for Hillsborough to see Wednesday, I'd be parking up at Bramall Lane to watch us play United, a great team that had fallen on hard times, and without doubt the biggest team in League One.

I stayed off the bike for a week after the Portsmouth game, just in case any Carlisle-related injuries decided to belatedly rear their heads. I also had one eye on the fixture list, as the rearrangement of the Crewe game postponed in January for Tuesday March 19 meant I had to take on three long rides in 11 days at the end of the month. There was also the fact that the weather was supposed to be improving as winter turned to spring, but that just wasn't happening, and throughout March and much of April 2013, England remained a resolutely bleak place to ride a bicycle.

I went out for a training ride the Thursday before Sheffield and felt really tight in my muscles, and I was lacking a little in confidence when I left very early on the Saturday morning. As it transpired, the ride started better than I expected, and the fact that I'd already done it once before was of great use as I again met Chris for a breakfast stop near Hinckley. As I left him to continue north, the weather turned a lot colder and a lot wetter. I'd checked the forecast before I left, so that didn't come as a huge surprise, but that didn't stop it giving me a serious chill.

My pace slowed down, to a mere shadow of the Bradley Wiggins time-trial pace I'd managed on my way to Portsmouth. I again travelled up through Derby, but steered clear of the A38 this time, heading up towards the town of Alfreton before setting a course for Chesterfield. I was bitterly cold and things were irritating me: roads that were closed for no apparent reason were a particular bugbear. Sir Dave Brailsford, the mastermind of British Cycling and Team Sky, calls it 'the chimp on your back', when bad things just mount up and things just don't seem like they're going to get better.

I was wasted by the time I reached Alfreton, and I took the relatively rare step of calling Margaret for a bit of moral support. I felt like I was just surviving, rather than really achieving something on two wheels, a feeling that I'd endured a fair few times over the course of the long British winter, but one that I never really acclimatised to. Mile after mile of misery whirred through my legs, up to and through Chesterfield, and then onto a more minor road up to Sheffield that cut out the stresses of the A61 traffic. I just wasn't in the mood for the A61 that day.

Maybe a bit of complacency had seeped into my mind after Carlisle. Maybe I'd started to think: "Well, that's the hard bit done, it's a piece of cake from here." Obviously, it wasn't, and that ride to Sheffield United was very much the slap in the face that taught me a very valuable lesson about taking the weather and my physical performance for granted.

I reached Bramall Lane eventually and their staff really

went the extra mile to get me back into a shape that vaguely resembled a human being. They'd reserved a room for me in the Copthorne Hotel, adjacent to the away end, where I could have a shower and a rest in comfort and privacy. As I wasn't too tight for time, I took this as an ideal opportunity to relax and warm up in a hot bath before bracing the cold once again for the match. The manager of the hotel met me at the door and took me up to the room they'd set aside, and after that he left me to my own devices to run a bath.

You know when you stay in a nice hotel and they've got some ridiculously complicated mixer tap on the bath that you can't bloody work out? You can probably see where this is going. On the one day that I really could have done with a hot bath, I couldn't fathom how to turn the tap to run hot water from it. I spent five minutes wrestling with the thing, after which my physical and mental tiredness got the better of me and I gave up. But I still needed a bath, so I ran a cold one and jumped into it. Not the cleverest thing in the world, I know, but I was too tired to think straight at that point. I tried to convince myself that it was the kind of 'ice bath' pro cyclists use to recover for the next day's race, but that was nonsense. It just made me feel even colder than I already was.

After a quick spot of lunch, I headed into the ground to watch an entertaining 0-0 draw in Sheffield for the second time in just over two months. United's striker Dave Kitson gave our back four grief throughout, but they managed to hold on, but things looked bad when our keeper Ian McLoughlin started hobbling around after diving to grab the ball and prevent a certain goal ten minutes from time. McLoughlin had little first-team experience, only really being called into the front line when regular 'keeper David Martin got injured up at Carlisle, and we had no substitute 'keeper on the bench. Backed by as much noise as the 400 Dons fans behind him could muster, the Irishman boldly held the Blades out for the last ten minutes to secure the draw, although that didn't help the Dons' fading play-off prospects, with the team struggling to stay in the top half of the table.

The following week, it began to snow again, and I started to believe that the curse of Crewe had struck for a second time. My next game, ten days after Sheffield United, was the rescheduled fixture at Crewe Alexandra, after the original game had been lost to heavy snow in January. Surely the same couldn't happen again?

The snow kept me from running any training rides during the week after the Sheffield United game, and even through the weekend, it still wasn't certain that my trip to Crewe would be on. I made it out onto my bike the day before the fixture and did a short 20-mile ride, just from home to Winslow and back, basically as a sort of systems check for my bike and my body after a relatively long period of time out of action. I came around a tightening blind corner on a quiet country road when I suddenly found my front wheel meeting a pothole full of water and topped in ice. Down I went. *Crunch*.

I skidded across the road on my bottom and into the verge on the far side. A car had been approaching from the other direction, but was able to stop in good time before unceremoniously piling into cycle or cyclist. I stood up, dusted myself off, remounted and gingerly rode away, kicking myself for coming out to ride in these conditions in the first place.

"What are you doing, Adam?! There's nothing for you to gain by coming out to ride today. You're going to get yourself hurt."

I returned home to find that the biggest injury I'd suffered was to my confidence. I'd suffered a few grazes on my legs from sliding along the road, but they were patched up reasonably easily. It was my first crash of the season, and indeed, it turned out to be my only crash of the season. But coming one day before a long ride to Crewe that would involve similar wintry hazards throughout, I didn't feel so sure of my capabilities and my safety as I had done previously. I guess I'd never really considered the possibility of a crash until it had actually happened.

As I came into the season run-in, I found myself riding many of the same routes again and again. From somewhere like Milton Keynes, which is relatively central in the country, I'd noticed that there were a few basic routes that would take me most of the way to any locations in a certain area of the country. Games in Yorkshire or the North-East would take me via the Markham Moor McDonalds, for example. In the case of fixtures held towards the North-West of England, the A5 and the Trent Valley to the east of Birmingham were very much my friends, and so I had no big surprises waiting for me as I travelled to Crewe (Tuesday March 19).

Following the same route I'd taken to Tranmere pretty much all the way (although without the cake and pork pie stop this time!), the ride was a good one and my worries about winter conditions or ending up on my arse again were quickly forgotten as I churned through the first few miles. Instead of meeting Chris on the A5 at High Cross near Hinckley, I saved him the effort and went to his house, not too far off-course in Rugby. Not to be outdone, Chris opened his front door and ushered me through to his living room, where he'd prepared a cyclist's dream breakfast: pot of tea, bacon roll, and highlights of that week's Paris-Nice race on the TV. Lovely man, that Chris.

As I carried on through rural Warwickshire, it suddenly dawned on me that for the first time since my ill-fated trip to Doncaster three months previously, I was riding north and I had a tailwind. With a smile on my face, I pushed on through past Tamworth, but took a minor wrong turn nearby. I didn't mind too much, though, as I reached a gated drive with a claret and blue badge adorning the front wall: I'd stumbled upon the Aston Villa training ground.

Never one to pass up on an opportunity, I decided to

hang around and see if I could meet any players. I whipped off my hi-vis gear to leave my MK Dons SET cycling top proudly displayed. It made me cold, so I was holding on shivering at the gates as a couple of players came through the gates to leave. Unfortunately, their cars all had smoked glass so I couldn't see any faces. Besides, they were probably wary of some juddering bloke in a bike helmet and MK Dons gear hanging around outside their training ground at 1:30pm on a Tuesday. In hindsight, I'd have been wary myself.

The rest of the ride was cold, but fairly easy, and I was making the most of the tailwind to carry on at a fair old pace. I reached Crewe's ground, Gresty Road, with plenty of time before the game, and went into the club shop to ask if I could take a quick picture. The man agreed, at which point I spotted a changing room. I enquired to see if I could use it, and the man said he'd go and check, which I thought was very odd: it was just a club shop changing room, after all.

As I was hanging around waiting for this bizarre permission, I was greeted by Steve Phillips, Crewe's goalkeeper. He clocked me in my cycling gear, and we struck up a lively conversation about cycling (see picture at the start of this chapter. It turned out that he was training to ride from London to Paris to raise money for prostate cancer research, and it was great to speak to someone who wasn't just paying me lip-service. He was genuinely interested in my experiences and keen to soak up every bit of training advice I could give him. I was happy to help.

After getting changed, and enjoying dinner from the best chip shop I've ever visited in my life (just near the top of Gresty Road, if you're ever in Crewe), I went for a quick pint in the bar at the Royal Hotel over the road, where most of the 140-odd Dons fans that had made the trip had gathered. I came in to find Tony and Dan sat at a table at the far end, arguing about whether or not the pub in question was an LGBT bar. Dan, who had directed most of the coach party to this pub, insisted it wasn't. Tony quipped that the neon lights and the bunch of squaddies in very convincing drag on a Tuesday night suggested otherwise. I personally don't think it was a gay bar, but watching two friends get out of their trees about something so petty gave me a bit of comic relief.

I needed that comic relief later on, when I was forced to endure the worst performance I saw the Dons put in all season. Dan assured me the Oldham game I'd missed in February was worse, but that this was, in his usual expletive-filled words, 'pretty f****** close'. A 1-0 half-time lead was quickly turned into a 2-1 defeat, and Antony Kay being sent off for the third time in the season was the icing on a not very nice cake. I felt for Karl Robinson that night, because you could see how much promotion slipping away was hurting him. At the end of the game, he made a point of shaking the hands of the linesmen and deliberately ignoring the hand of the referee, who he blamed for the red card and a host of other contentious decisions. At least Robinson cared, I thought.

The return of snow later that week didn't cheer me up much, especially I was facing the very real prospect of a 100-mile ride right through it to Colchester United that Saturday (March 23). It was another marginal call as to whether the game was going to be on. Particularly heavy snow was forecast for Friday night and Saturday morning, but obviously referees can't call a game off until the snow has actually come down and the pitch is deemed unplayable. This is all perfectly sensible stuff, but didn't help me, what with needing to leave home before 8:00am on the Saturday morning to reach the north Essex club's Weston Homes Community Stadium in time for the game (assuming there was one).

Late on Friday night, I packed everything up and resolved that I was going to at least try to get there. I wasn't looking forward to it. I'd chosen to ride my old steel-framed bike rather than my carbon-bodied beauty, because it had a bit more give in difficult situations. And I didn't want to ruin my pride and joy in such rubbish weather.

I awoke early on Saturday, around 6:30am, to find that very little snow had actually settled on the ground, and that there was only sleet in the air. Then I took my dog out for a quick walk and slipped over three times before I reached the end of my road. I muttered to myself: "I'm not cycling 100 miles through this."

Back indoors, I fired up my phone to see if I'd got any correspondence from Colchester's media officer, with whom I'd been conversing about the impending bad weather all week. At about 8:00am, the time I realistically needed to leave, he texted me to say that he was on his way to the stadium to check the conditions, but I was running short of time and was quickly coming around to the conclusion that this wasn't worth attempting. It was simply a bridge too far for me. But I remained in my kit by my phone waiting for news, in case I had to jump on my bike straight away and start making up for lost time if the game had been declared on.

He rang at 9:00am to say that no official decision had been made, but that most of Essex was covered in snow and he couldn't see a way the game was going to be played. By that time, I had to either leave for Colchester or decide I wasn't going to try it. I chose the latter, a decision justified by the official postponement of the game at 10:05am. It was a hellish Saturday saved, but it meant another Tuesday trek piled on towards the end of the season.

The following week, the weather improved as Easter approached. The long winter hadn't quite released its vice-like grip on the UK just yet, but had loosened it a little, enough to at least eliminate the possibility of any more snow. I had four rides left, including the rescheduled Colchester match. That, and the two others scheduled for April weren't likely to cause me too many issues. But before that, I was headed to the far north once again for my last two-day adventure. Good Friday meant Hartlepool.

CHAPTER 9: WHY I RIDE

Hartlepool was, metaphorically, the final mountain that I had to climb. It was the last two-day ride I'd have to face, taking me more than 200 miles north to the small town on the sea between Sunderland and Middlesbrough. It was going to be tough, but after everything I'd faced on the previous 24 rides, I was well-prepared for it. There was no snow, but the weather was still cold – only two or three degrees above freezing all the way there. On top of that, the evil headwind had returned, and would blow at more than 15mph pretty much all the way there.

With the game being played on Good Friday afternoon (March 29), I left home first thing on the Thursday morning, with the intention of reaching the same Holiday Inn in Leeds where I'd put a dent into the EU lasagne mountain en route to Carlisle five weeks previously. I wouldn't be riding to Leeds, though: the intention was to ride to York, where Chris would bundle me and the bike into his car, drive me to the hotel, and then drive me back to York to resume the next morning. Leeds was the nearest hotel in which Sarah had been able to secure me a room, but I had a long enough ride ahead of me already without adding on extra miles through West Yorkshire.

The first 50 miles took me as far as Kettering and my usual rendezvous with Chris. I felt excellent, especially as I knew that Chris was going to follow me from there all the way to Hartlepool. Although cold, the sun was shining and I felt like I was making good time, even though the wind was in my face, and I thoroughly enjoyed my wrap and coffee at McDonald's in Kettering. I'd wheeled my bike into McDonald's with me, which was something I always did at any of my pit-stops, but this was a little different. I'd barely sat down when a woman I assumed was the manageress came striding straight up to me. I thought she was going to inform me that: "Bicycles are not permitted in McDonald's Restaurant. Please lock it up on the fence outside. Thank you." But as she approached, she had a wry grin on her face.

"Keep one hand on that bike," she said. "They'll nick anything around here. They even nick the light bulbs out of the toilets." I couldn't help but laugh.

On from Kettering and through Corby and Oakham once again, the cold was beginning to wear me down, to the point that I had to stop for a short time to try and recoup a bit of energy. The day was starting to slowly grind me down, and nothing I ate or drank was able to stop me from getting a sinking feeling, but I kept on at a steady if unspectacular pace until I reached the McDonald's at Markham Moor once again. I spent 90 minutes there before I resumed, because it took me that long to warm up to a level where I didn't feel uncomfortable getting back onto the bike.

Eventually I did so, but the whole trip just started to feel samey around this time. Long straight A-roads along pan-flat terrain, punctuated by the occasional identikit roundabout on the occasional identikit bypass around the occasional identikit town. People say most of Milton Keynes looks the same: try the northern parts of Nottinghamshire and Lincolnshire.

As I reached Doncaster, I started to feel ill (and no, I'm sure it had nothing to do with visiting McDonald's twice in the same day). My stomach started to turn, to the point where vomit was coming up into my mouth and I was having to swallow it back down. All the while, I was still pedalling. I couldn't stop. Feeling as I did and with the cold as it was, there was a very good chance that I just wouldn't have got started again if I'd stopped.

It had been a very long day already, but I gamely tried to reach York, around 160 miles from Milton Keynes and a huge amount of riding to take on in one day. To put it into perspective, that's longer than most of the stages on the Tour de France. OK, there weren't any Alps in the way and I wasn't racing anyone, but then I'm not a professional cyclist – I'm a mere environmental consultant!

I tried to take in more energy, but every time I tried to swallow anything even remotely sugary, it came straight back up within seconds. Even sipping drinks as gently as I could resulted in the same effect. I carried on through South Yorkshire, mercifully on a section that was mostly downhill, but then my lights started to flash, indicating that they were low on battery. As it was past 6:00pm by this point, it was completely dark and the road ahead became an even bigger challenge than it already was.

I got as far as Selby with my flickering lights before I finally threw in the towel. "Sod trying to get to York," I gasped to Chris. "Just put me in the car and take me to Leeds. We'll start again from here tomorrow." We went straight to the Holiday Inn and emulated my carb-loading that I'd undergone there on the Carlisle trip. I literally scoffed as much lasagne and garlic bread as you could fit on the table. But my problems with getting food down hadn't stopped, and it took me an hour and a half to clear the plates. I felt utterly exhausted, to the point that even lifting a fork to my mouth felt like a chore.

I felt mentally and physically low when I went to bed that night, and although I tried to gee myself up with the bright, sunny start to Good Friday, I restarted from Selby in a very negative frame of mind. "I don't want to be here," I murmured to Chris, who I could see was sympathetic to my plight but wasn't quite sure what he could say to help. I was so down that if he'd offered to put me into the car and drive me to the edge of Hartlepool before dropping me off for the finish, I probably would have said: "Go on, we'll get away with it." Sensibly, he didn't, and off we went through the various villages that led us to North Yorkshire.

That was the one moment where I felt a real pang of empathy with professional bike riders facing multi-day marathons such as the Tour de France. When you've had one real tough day on the bike and just want to relax, you still have to scoop yourself out of bed the next morning, drag that aching leg over the crossbar, clip your feet onto the pedals and start riding again. Every part of your body doesn't want you to do it, but your mind tells those rebellious body parts that they have to comply.

I started to ride from village to village, treating them like a series of short time-trials. I couldn't think about the next bit, or the bit after. I was treating it like it was a five-mile blast on the cycle racing circuit that runs around the National Bowl in Milton Keynes, a place where I sometimes race during the summer months. As long as I kept things nice and steady, I had nothing to be afraid of. I'd brought my aero bars with me, a pair of hand-grips that attach to the middle of the handlebar and protrude forwards over the front wheel. By holding them, my body had a narrower profile, making me more aerodynamically efficient against the wind and making my job just that little bit easier. Fed up of battering the headwind with my shoulders, I put them onto the bike for the second day and pretended I had a yellow jersey on my back.

Even restarting from Selby rather than York, I only had another 60 miles or so to cover to reach Hartlepool. I was going to take the high road over the North York Moors to get there, but I'd heard there was still plenty of snow on the uppermost roads and opted to head around it instead. Chris and I made brief stops at York Minster and York City Football Club, before we hit the A19. It's sometimes the little things that cheer you up, and as I left the outskirts of York, the sign to Hartlepool gave me confidence that the end was in sight.

For a main road, the A19 to Thirsk was surprisingly kind to me. It was a straight road, with wide lanes and was devoid of traffic all the way up. As I started to get closer to Thirsk and the edge of the Moors, the road started undulating more, which had a really positive effect as it allowed me to stretch out my muscles properly and start to enjoy bike riding and life in general once again. I stopped at a small café in the town square at Thirsk, not only to enjoy a cup of tea but to map out the route ahead, with Chris's help. There were several different options, although the A19, which became a dual carriageway here as it filtered traffic away from the A1, stood out as the quickest option. I thought, on the basis that it was early in the morning on a Bank Holiday and there wouldn't be enough traffic to make things uncomfortable, that it would be fine.

We left the café and for the first time on that trip, I felt really confident and happy. I realised as soon as I turned onto the A19 that I was going to need every scrap of that confidence. It was busy. Really busy. At one stage, I was being passed by a large grain lorry, just as another one was coming down the slip-road to my left. For a moment, I was the very squishy meat in a very solid sandwich.

"I just hope they've seen me," I thought. "If this is going to be the end, I want it to end quickly and without pain."

They had seen me, and they both slotted into line in front. The whole thing was over in a flash, but the experience was enough to make me want to not be on the A19 any longer. At the next lay-by, I stopped to call Chris to work out an alternative route, and by luck, he'd parked up on the bridge on the turn-off just ahead. He'd obviously been unable to follow right behind me on a busy dual carriageway, and so was driving ahead in sections at normal car speeds. As he was just ahead, I rode the last couple of hundred metres and met him on the bridge.

We decided that, as neither of us had been on it before and as we had time on our side, that we should head for Middlesbrough and cross the Tees on the famous Transporter Bridge. An incredible piece of great British engineering, it consists of two huge tower crane-like steel structures, one on each bank, that are connected in the middle. A platform, known as the 'cradle', is suspended from them on strong cables, and that cradle carries pedestrians, bikes and road traffic from one side of the Tees to the other.

Our route also meant that we could pop by another football ground, so we worked our way along the minor A-roads to Middlesbrough FC's Riverside Stadium. When we arrived, I quickly popped into the club shop and bought myself a Middlesbrough badge before heading towards the Transporter Bridge. We noticed that there were some pretty strong gusts blowing along the Tees estuary, and we knew that the bridge was normally closed in strong winds for safety reasons. Initially, looking over from the stadium, we couldn't see the cradle making its trips back and forth across the river. As a safeguard, Chris and I came up with a Plan B of travelling all the way round to the other side of the bridge by car, unloading me and my bike there, and then continuing to Hartlepool. Although we weren't tight for time, the big detour we'd have to take if the bridge was closed would have caused a bit of a strain if cycled.

As I rode along the short road up to the bridge, it started to hail and snow, seemingly at the same time. Bands of snow were snaking across the road, but incredibly, the bridge had remained open, and was just waiting for a couple more passengers to arrive. The cheery attendant waved us onto the bridge, and we were off over the wide open seaward Tees in dreadful conditions. We felt like a couple of six-year-olds on an old steam train, as if our parents had taken us on a day out to do something really cool. We loved it, taking plenty of pictures before we disembarked. Considering how low I had felt the day before, the short trip on that fine example of British industrial heritage somehow made the whole trip for me.

Miraculously, the snow stopped and the sun came out as we started up again on the northern side of the Tees. There were only a few miles to rattle off before we rolled into Hartlepool and pulled up at United's tiny ground, Victoria Park. It was the perfect weather for me to complete a ride that had given me a huge sense of achievement. Granted, it was a ride roughly 50 miles shorter than that to Carlisle, but I'd had to battle extremely changeable conditions, with a cold headwind as well as illness, making it just as tortuous a trek as my ride to Cumbria in many ways.

The club kindly gave me a ball signed by all the players for my charity raffle, and I then walked past the away end into The Corner Flag, the main supporters' bar. An odd two-storey brick building, away fans are allowed in on payment of a 50p entrance fee, and are then treated to their own bar and lounge area upstairs. It's a proper old-school club bar, as well – think of the cabaret suite in *Peter Kay's Phoenix Nights* and you'll get a rough idea of what it's like. Downstairs was another bar, reserved for the Hartlepool supporters, past which were the toilets, into which I headed to get changed.

I gave myself a quick wash in the sink as I got changed into rather less sweaty gear and had just about finished when one of the Corner Flag staff came in and asked me if I'd like a shower. I wasn't really that keen, because I'd already sorted myself out, but I didn't want to offend them after they'd gone to the trouble of offering me one, and so he led me into the shower room.

"It's the first time anyone's ever used this shower," the man said excitedly. "It was installed for the supporters' team about ten years ago, but no-one's ever used it." There was no way I could refuse with a story like that, but having been there for so long, said shower wasn't working very well. Within seconds, four Hartlepool fans were crammed into this shower room, desperately trying to get the thing to work, but the water would only come out either scalding hot or freezing cold. There was absolutely no setting in between which would allow me (or anyone, for that matter) to enjoy a pleasant, refreshing shower. On top of that, there was no shower curtain in the room. Or working light. Or lock on the door. But nonetheless I tried, and plumped for the scalding hot option while four large men guarded the door lest someone unexpectedly caught me in the nip. The whole thing was a disaster, but it was so nice of them to really try to get it working. Of all the sets of fans that I met on my travels, the Hartlepool fans were the warmest and kindest of the lot.

I got dry and dressed, and climbed the stairs to the away bar. I could hear Dan, Tony and the like cheering every time someone they knew walked through the door, or so I assumed. It turned out they were waiting for me, and each time the door opened, an expectant 'woooooooah' was followed by a disappointed 'oooooh' as someone who wasn't me came into the room with a bemused look on his or her face (apparently, Nicola got this treatment twice, much to her amusement). Then I came in and they practically cheered the picture frames off the walls, and all I could do was laugh out loud.

After shaking everybody's hands, Chris placed a pint into my hand and said something particularly poignant to me. Chris isn't a Dons fan and so was unused to the community spirit that comes among our away supporters, and he noticed something particularly telling.

"You've got a group of 50-60 people in here that you know who come away on days like this for a great day out," he said. "It doesn't even seem like the football is the be-all and end-all – it's all about having fun with your mates, like a big extended family." And I thoroughly enjoyed being amongst that family as the Dons finally recorded their first away win in the League since New Year's Day. It wasn't too much to shout about – Hartlepool were bottom of the table and almost certain to be relegated to League Two – but 2-0 away wins were like hen's teeth to us, and I very much made the most of it.

Coming home, I tried to work out how tough Hartlepool had been compared to Carlisle. Yes, Hartlepool was tough with weather and illness, but it was a good deal shorter and the ride to Carlisle had just gone on and on, almost without end. I don't think anything could compare to Carlisle.

And so I entered April, the final month of the season, in which I'd complete my last three rides. There was no doubt that I'd complete them, either – the combined distance of the trio was shorter than the trip to Hartlepool on its own. This allowed me to divert my attentions slightly into organising a grand finale for the last day of the season, which I'll come back to later.

The month began with a home game against Crawley on Saturday April 6 (a goalless draw that really did kill off our chances of making the play-offs, Ryan Lowe having three goals disallowed). But the day had been designated a special event for disability sports teams in the area. There had been a disabled junior football tournament held at a nearby secondary school on the morning of the game tied into the whole thing, to which I was happy to pay a visit. These were exactly the people that my fundraising was helping, and the numbers of players' parents that came up to me to thank me for my efforts was simply heart-warming. I'd just about reached my revised target of £5000 by this stage, and the half that the SET was due to receive was bound to go an incredibly long way in buying kit and equipment.

STADIUM CHASE

With the school in between my home and stadium:mk, I rode there and then on to the stadium, bizarrely making it the only home game of the entire season to which I'd travelled on two wheels. The bike was then called into action at half-time for a parade of the players from that tournament. Well, it was once a jobsworth steward who tried to stop me taking it in had been pulled aside – it almost led to a "don't you know who I am?" moment, which would have been my one full-scale 'diva strop' of the whole season. As the first half ended, we duly made our way out onto the red walkway that separates the stadium:mk pitch from the stands.

Everyone seemed incredibly proud to be there, but as we came around towards the away end (and a kind, appreciative set of Crawley supporters), I noticed one young lad on crutches was struggling to keep up. He was desperately trying to stay with the group because he was enjoying his day in the limelight so much, but he just wasn't physically able to complete the lap of the pitch. I collared the person next to him and quickly said: "Put him on the bike." Being only a small lad, this wasn't too difficult, and he sat on the saddle as I held the handlebars and wheeled him around the dugout and the Cowshed home end.

I thought nothing of it at the time. But at the end of the following week, just as I was about to leave for my next ride to Leyton Orient, a letter came through the post from the boy's father. He thanked me for helping the boy out with transport, and that the lad had been so excited that all he'd talked about all week was how he'd gone on Adam's racing bike. It inspired me all the way to East London, via the Arsenal training ground (where a burly guard escorted me into the car park to take a picture of the entrance sign, and then immediately escorted me out again, so tight was the security there) and Tottenham Hotspur's ground, White Hart Lane.

From there I travelled via the Emirates Stadium, the

matchday home of Arsenal, and with the Gunners playing there that day, I couldn't believe how many people were around. OK, I knew that every Arsenal home game was pretty much a 60,000 sell-out, but every single pub I passed within what seemed like a three-mile radius of the stadium was crammed, with people spilling out five deep onto the pavement. I shuddered to think of the amount of money being spent just in the pubs that day – probably enough for Karl Robinson to buy an entire new Dons squad!

As I reached Brisbane Road, Orient's charming old-fashioned ground, it had just started to hail, making me thankful that I'd left early enough to dodge the worst of the weather for once. Orient had nowhere for me to change, so I resorted to the team bus again, and went in to watch us lose 2-0 to a brace of goals in the last ten minutes from a team that would ultimately finish just ahead of us in the table.

There was very much an end-of-term atmosphere around the club, the fans and the rides by this point. It seemed as if the Dons would recover to finish in the top ten, but we knew we'd be short of the sixth place required to get us into the play-offs. This made for a much more relaxed, and dare I say it, fun vibe to everything, and that was certainly the case for my penultimate ride.

The Tuesday after Orient (April 16), I cycled the 100 miles to the game at Colchester United, the one that had been postponed due to snow three weeks previously. I left stadium:mk at about 1:00pm on a bright, sunny and (surprisingly) warm day, heading east across the Bedfordshire and Hertfordshire countryside. Before I picked up the A120, which would take me due east, passing Stansted Airport en route to Colchester, I stopped for a half-time break, and saw that my average speed had again romped past 20mph. "I'm going to arrive way too early here," I thought. But I couldn't help it, as it was a relatively flat route, ideal for a high-speed ride, and it wasn't tiring me out a great deal.

I focused on trying to reach the ground in under five hours, which therefore would give me an 20mph-plus average for the whole day. Apart from a small ford in a village (which gave me flashbacks to the Newark flood in December) and two geese that tried to side-swipe me off my bike, there was nothing in my way to slow me down. I achieved my five-hour goal comfortably (four hours 41 minutes), and came into the Westom Homes Community Stadium to be greeted by Colchester's chairman, Robbie Cowling, running into the stadium. I'd seen on the BBC's local football show *Late Kick-Off* that he was training for a charity ride to Carlisle of his own, as his team had been handed the long trip to the Cumbrians on the last day of the season, which by this stage was just 11 days away.

After getting a photo with him (below), Cowling gave me my own changing room (next to the first-team changing room), and I scuttled around to the away section watch the Dons record an impressive if meaningless 2-0 win against a team struggling to avoid relegation (they would manage it in the end).

That extremely competitive ride (my Strava page for that day is littered with top-ten times) had finished my long-distance efforts for the season, and left me with just one more ride to go, which also happened to be the shortest of them all. My adventure, which at times I thought was impossible, was almost complete.

CHAPTER 10: THE FINAL STAGE

Just 34 miles from Milton Keynes, Stevenage was my destination for the last game of the season, on Saturday April 27. Mindful that it was my last chance to get myself into the public consciousness and raise more cash (until Dan came up with the idea of writing this book), I was determined to pull out all the stops to make it an extra-special day.

Throughout the eight-month season, I was keen to keep things fresh and interesting for potential donors. The last thing I wanted was for people to look at me and think: "Oh, he's done another ride". And with Stevenage being such a short trip, it gave me the ideal opportunity to get people involved. Aside from Coventry in early October, I'd ridden to all the other games on my own, and quite a few people, some cyclists and some football fans, had asked if they could join me on the trip to Stevenage. It made sense for me to make it an open ride.

If I was going to get so many people involved, I had to get organised and do things properly. I registered it with British Cycling as a Reliability Ride, which meant I could organise entries through the BC website, secure rider insurance and potentially attract other cyclists in the local area to join. There's always costs to organising events, so I opened entries around eight weeks beforehand, asking for

£5 per person. As the day drew nearer, around 60 people had signed up, many of whom had no interest in football and so would ride from stadium:mk to Stevenage's ground, Broadhall Way, and then simply turn around and ride back without staying for the game.

But around 20 people were simply going to Stevenage and staying on for the game, some of whom were friends from Leighton Buzzard Road Cycling Club, and some of whom were just hardy enthusiasts. Given that they'd be cycling at vastly different speeds, I set the ride up so that the slower riders would leave earlier, and that we'd all muster at a pub in Whitwell, a village a few miles short of Stevenage, from where everyone would enjoy a swift half and ride to Broadhall Way together. What would make that stop even more enticing was that Dons away regular Radar had organised a pub stop coach full of fans to call at the same place. And as it was the last day of the season, fancy dress was the order of the day, so they'd all be dressed as nuns. Nice.

That went down very well with the police, who obviously had to make sure that everyone stayed under control (not that MK Dons fans have any history of significant trouble). They were much happier having everyone in the same place rather than trying to oversee two completely separate groups in different places. The pub's landlady wasn't as keen, but as a businesswoman she couldn't turn down a huge influx of business on an otherwise-quiet Saturday lunchtime. Meanwhile, the local Honda Goldwing club had got involved and agreed to escort the riders through the countryside, and the Mayor of Milton Keynes, Cllr Catriona Morris, was to follow us in her mayoral car.

It's worth explaining just how the mayor came to be involved with my project. Milton Keynes mayors are elected by their peers on the council for one-year terms, and they are each allowed to nominate a local charity to be the beneficiary of all their fundraising work over their 12 months in charge. Catriona, as a passionate Dons fan often seen at away games (in the stands rather than the hospitality boxes), had chosen the MK Dons SET when she became mayor in May 2012.

It was when she attended my launch two days before I rode to Cheltenham last August that I got to talk to her. I'd previously worked in local government, so I'd had to deal with mayors before, and I'd found them to be a vapid lot that would smile and nod at what you had to say without taking a blind bit of notice of what you were actually saying. Catriona was different. She seemed genuinely interested in what I was doing to help, even to the point of lifting my bike to see just how light it was, and came across as someone knowledgeable and proactive.

We kept in touch throughout the season, and we bumped into each other again when she came to the Sheffield Wednesday FA Cup game at Hillsborough in early January. The first thing she asked me was: "Have you reached your £1000 target?" When I'd replied that I'd already raised more than double that, she was stunned. After that, she invited me to her civic reception and honoured me with an award for my fundraising, and an off-the-cuff comment of mine that she should follow us on the last ride quickly turned into a serious plan. Her help has been invaluable, and I'm sure that some of her contacts have helped generate extra income for my fund. As a contact to have in the Milton Keynes area, you couldn't ask for a better one.

As April 27 approached, it was really starting to feel like I was doing something big, even though the ride would represent just over one per cent of my total mileage for the season. The week leading up to the game took up all of my free time as all the plans made for the day needed to be put in place. For example, I had to spend 15 hours going along the route putting signposts up so that people wouldn't get lost (and another 15 the following week taking them all down again). Hooning around the back lanes of

STADIUM CHASE

Hertfordshire at 11:00pm wasn't particularly fun, and I was actually glad to be rid of all that hard work by the time the day itself came around.

The cold but reasonably dry final day of the season started early, around 7:00am, with the Dons agreeing to open one section of stadium:mk to give us a dry place for us to sign everyone in. Chaineys Cycles, the bike shop of my dreams from last summer, sent a representative to give everyone's bikes a free check-up before they left, and everything went fairly smoothly to begin with.

The first 'slower' group of ten left at around 8:00am, and contained the kind of people who weren't big on cycling but were riding (and in some cases had raised their own money for my fund) just to help me. One was Gio, a disabled Dons season fan who was a keen handbike rider. He'd wanted to join me on a ride all season, but every time he was free to do so, the ride was either too long for him or too wet or snow-swept for him to be completely safe. Another was Robert Quirke, another Dons fan who went out of his way repeatedly to give me support all year, and had actually been one of my biggest donors, giving me £100 as soon as I announced what I was doing the previous summer.

The second 'medium-paced' group left at 9:00am, and this contained the majority of riders, with only me and my LBRCC team-mates staying to bomb it down in the fast group. This medium group contained Bobby Winkelman, Dons team scout and son of chairman Pete. Bobby was using it as a warm-up for rowing the English Channel for a separate charity cause the following day, but turned up with a knackered old mountain bike that practically gave the man from Chaineys a heart attack when he came to tune it up. It also contained a fellow fan of mine, Ross Gallacher, who had probably made the biggest effort of all to take part.

Ross is a young Scotsman who had been to every game home and away over the course of the season; he was a panellist on the MK Dons Radio Show and has become a firm friend of mine. Ross wanted to use the ride as motivation to get himself into shape. He attended spin classes at his local gym a couple of times a week, but had zero road cycling experience, and had never sat on a racing bike in his life. He took things so seriously that he spent two months immersed in training for what I thought was a fairly simple and leisurely 34-mile ride, and even set up his own JustGiving page, similar to my own, so he could raise his own money to add to my fund. Incredibly, he raised £300 in the end. Not bad at all for a man who started off petrified of riding on the road.

In the couple of weeks before the game, Ross had visited me and I'd given him some tuition on riding on the road, and that he had nothing to fear from a bike with such skinny tyres. He also joined a beginners session at LBRCC to get used to riding in a group. Those sessions swiftly improved his confidence to such an extent that we bumped him up from the slow group to the medium group for Stevenage, as I was fully confident that he wouldn't get left behind, hold anyone up or cause any problems due to his inexperience.

Then it was my turn to depart. The riders that remained all lined up in the car park, with the mayor and the Goldwings lined up in formation for some photos we could send to the local press, and then suddenly, off we went. Most of the motorbikes (one of which was carrying Margaret on the back) went ahead, blocking off junctions so that a group of our size could pass through safely (if any policemen or women are reading this, they didn't actually block the road. But it was nice that the cars slowed down to let us out!). The mayor's car slotted in behind, carrying both her and Dan, whom I'd wanted to get to see the ride for reference for this book. Never one to pass up on a chance to blur the lines of gender (maybe that pub at Crewe *was* a gay bar!), Dan had still adhered to Radar's fancy dress rules, and so rode with the mayor in full nun costume. Funnily enough, the mayor didn't seem to mind.

Soon after my 'fast' peloton left Milton Keynes, the heavens opened, with a short, sharp blast of rain and hail peppering the roads. But those roads were brightened up by the bright LED lights and blaring country-and-western music attached to the brash 'pimped' Goldwings. Dan remarked later that with so many cars and motorbikes around, it looked like a real stage of the Tour de France, and he also remarked that when we reached the only steep climb of the route, around the halfway mark, I seemed to 'attack' and pulled away from the other riders behind. I was enjoying having riders with me, but I just wanted to have a few moments out on the front with Margaret (who was on the lead motorbike). The success of this project is as much down to her tolerance and support as anything else.

There was also some serious intent to my breakaway: many of the Goldwings had pulled away and left us behind. I knew they were all connected up to each other via an intercom system, so I raced up to one of them to tell them to slow down. After an intercom discussion, they agreed that it just wasn't practical for them to slow even further and come down to cyclist pace, so we agreed that they should go on ahead to Whitwell and that we'd meet them there. They'd done a sterling job blocking off the early junctions through southern Milton Keynes, and we were now far enough out into the countryside that we'd be able to get along fine without them.

Over the last few miles before reaching Whitwell, I took pride of place at the front of what remained of the peloton (of the 12 other riders that had left MK in the 'fast' group, only seven had been able to stick with me). We rolled into Whitwell to a round of applause from cyclists and nuns alike, and pretty much everyone I wanted to see was there... except Ross. It had been one of my biggest concerns that morning: Ross getting separated from the group, misreading the signs and floating around the Hertfordshire countryside on his own. Given the chilly, changeable weather, that was the last thing I wanted.

I found Tony and John, his co-panellists on the radio show (neither of whom were dressed as nuns), to see if they had any idea where he was. But the moment I uttered the words: "We think Ross is lost", they just burst into laughter that was as hysterical as it was unhelpful. I found Margaret to see if she could help, and as I did, a huge cheer went up from the car park out front as a somewhat exasperated Ross wheeled in. The pub emptied as everyone poured into the car park to congratulate/tease him (delete as applicable). Ross works for Network Rail and therefore is frequently associated with trains, and so when a mildly inebriated nun started singing: "Just like his trains, he's ten minutes late" and everyone joined in, I hope he took it in the kind way it was intended. He didn't look especially pleased about it at the time.

Bobby Winkelman had come in with Ross and explained how they'd both got lost, missing one crucial arrow and ending up several miles away just outside Hitchin. To their credit, they managed to retrace their trail and got back onto the route at the point where they'd initially gone the wrong way. But they were here, and everything was back on plan, much to my relief.

It was at the pub that the financial benefits of making such a big deal out of the Stevenage trip began to become apparent. Dan grabbed an empty Pimm's jug and went around bullying any nuns he could find into donating whatever cash they had, and within three minutes filled said jug with £73. One of the women from the Goldwing club did the same, in a much kinder way, to anyone who wasn't dressed as a nun and simultaneously raised a similar amount.

At 12:30pm, it was time for us to leave Whitwell and cover the remaining five miles to Stevenage. Those five miles were a blur, but I remember everyone making the effort to stay together in one big pack. It reminded me of the final stage of the Tour de France each year, where the team of the winning rider all get the honour of riding at the front of the peloton before the mad dash up and down the Champs-Elysees begins. I went up onto the front of the group alongside Gio, from Knebworth right into Stevenage, and looking back and seeing that huge bunch behind me was a truly moving feeling. As we approached the ground, the heavy traffic made things a little tricky, but we pulled into the Broadhall Way car park soon enough. The finish.

I'd assured Stevenage FC that there wouldn't be bikes and cyclists strewn all over and getting in the way when we arrived, but that proved unavoidable on the day. We were also greeted by a significant contingent of Stevenage fans, who it turned out had been tipped off by Dan on their internet forum two days beforehand, and some of them had gone onto my JustGiving page to make donations. Some of them had lined Broadhall Way itself to applaud us as we rode past, but I had such tunnel-vision that day that I didn't even notice them.

As I stood there astride my stationary bike in the Stevenage car park, with cyclists and fans happily socialising around me, it felt like a truly fitting end to one of the greatest adventures of my life. It felt like I had achieved something genuinely meaningful, and that all the sweat and tears (and thankfully not very much blood) that had gone into the previous eight months was truly worthwhile. I'd made a promise, I'd stuck to it, and I'd given help to a huge number of Dons fans less fortunate than myself along the way.

The rest of that final afternoon sped by. After more photos with the mayor and the Goldwing crew in the car park, I nipped over to the team coach to get changed and stow my bike, while the other riders stashed their gear in the bus I'd laid on to return them to stadium:mk after the match. After I got changed, I was stood outside with Chris, the man who had fed me countless breakfasts, who had followed me to Carlisle and Hartlepool, and who had seen me at my very worst over the course of the season. We walked across to the stadium, and all we could say to each other was: "How mad was that?"

As I fumbled through my kitbag, my hand fell upon a bottle of champagne I'd brought for the occasion, and I came around the corner to find Margaret down the path in front of me. She wasn't best pleased at the idea of me dousing her in Moet, so I just sprayed it at the general vicinity. Some of the nuns got covered, which I'm sure they didn't mind one bit, and then I went into the ground to watch the game. Even then, I still had things to do. BBC Three Counties Radio rang me for an end-of-season interview, and then I got a tap on the shoulder: "Karl wants to see you."

A few minutes later, I found myself on the pitch having my picture taken with Robinson as I gratefully received the not insubstantial amount of money (around £350) that he'd collected from his players. Eventually, amid an alleyway of back-slaps and well-dones, I found my way to my seat (not that I was sitting in it – I was stood with the best of them) and watched the final game of our season.

About ten minutes into the game, I started to tot up all the money I'd received that day from a host of different sources. I'd begun that day having raised just over £5000, but thanks to Ross's donations, the Dons players, the Pimm's jug and countless other fivers and tenners here and there, I'd reached £6789. Excited, I swung my head round to find someone with whom I could share this information. I scanned across, one block to my left and about three rows behind. I saw John and Tony, then Tony's daughter Zoe wearing a nun's head-dress, and then a tall man in aviator sunglasses, wearing a nun's habit minus the head-dress. It could only be Dan. Only he would carry so little dress sense as to wear aviators while dressed as a nun.

I held up five fingers and a thumb at him to denote

'six', before slowly raising further fingers to indicate the 'seven', 'eight' and 'nine'. He knew what I meant straight away, and stared back at me open-mouthed in astonishment. You know that bit in *Top Gun* where Maverick and Goose have just spotted the hot girl and lower their sunglasses in astonishment? Imagine that, in a football ground, on a much lower budget, with a nun. That pretty much summed up Dan's reaction. Pleased with that measure of approval, I settled into the game, which we won 2-0. I wasn't best pleased that we'd only won six of 23 League away games that season, but at least we secured eighth place in the final table with 70 points.

Although my actual riding was completed (final distance 2975 miles – would have been over 3000 if I'd got to bloody Yeovil), donations continued to pour in for a number of weeks afterwards. By mid-May, as Yeovil beat Brentford in the play-off final to join Doncaster and Bournemouth in securing promotion to the Championship, my total had passed £8000. By that point, the total had risen by more than £2500 since the morning of the Stevenage game, which vindicated my plan to make a big deal out of the grand finale. And given that I'd set out exactly a year previously to cycle 1000 miles and raise £1000, it was a simply astonishing amount of money to have generated.

One man who rode with us to Stevenage raised £600 and got it matched by his employer, giving me another £1200. Another rider had given me a brand-new iPhone to add to my end-of-season raffle, a raffle which generated several hundred pounds in itself through the armada of prizes that I'd accrued on my travels. The generosity of people who had really identified with what I was doing is something I will never, ever forget.

Margaret and I drove home on that sunny evening, and as I settled down on the sofa, I could properlyrelax, for the first time in nearly nine months. Laying back, I closed my eyes and said: "It's done."

EPILOGUE

As I write this final chapter, the 2013/2014 season is about to commence. This time last year, I was looking forward to heading off to Cheltenham for the first game of last season, and worrying about the big 130-mile trip to Bournemouth that followed shortly after. The mighty Alan Smith had joked as I left stadium:mk for Cheltenham that I had an easy one to start with. Although I didn't think a 70-mile trip across the Cotswolds seemed particularly easy, he was eventually proved right.

If you'd asked me last August how my adventure would turn out, I couldn't have imagined it any better. The £8107 raised (not including the profits from sales of this book) has made a significant difference to the MK Dons SET's disability teams and to the Redway School. I got home safely from each ride, and the support from I received was tremendous - not only from fans and staff of MK Dons, but from fans and staff of countless other clubs, too.

What was the highlight? It has to be that final ride into Stevenage. The madness of that day will live on in my memory for the rest of my life. But there were plenty of other moments to savour: the trip to Doncaster to watch nothing (honestly!), the donation of over £700 from the Dons fans that travelled to Sheffield Wednesday, and of course, those snow-covered hills en route to Carlisle.

I've been hugely honoured by the response of clubs, fans and media alike to all this, but much like football, cycling is a team sport. In the case of the Tour de France (which is finishing as I write this), Chris Froome gets all the glory but Richie Porte and his Team Sky team-mates are the ones that work the hardest to aid him. In my case, those are all the people behind the scenes who weren't riding bikes. This hasn't been a professional venture by any means, but the attitude and support given by the cast of hundreds has been every bit as good as any professional team could enjoy (hence the long list of acknowledgements!).

Every person I've spoken to since the end has asked me the same thing: "What are you doing this season, then?" There have been plenty of suggestions. I'm not one for dressing up as a rhino and running the London Marathon (although I did the like someone suggested of dressing up at Donny and unicycling to games), because for me, it is all about the sport. I regard this as a massive personal sporting achievement. I didn't have the opportunity or the drive when I was young enough to achieve sporting success at the highest level, but this has shown me that it's never too late to get better at what you do. You just have to be a bit bloody-minded and have the right people around you.

The thing about cycling is that there is always another challenge. There are lots of records out there to be broken, and as this season marks the tenth anniversary of MK Dons, I have a great reason to try and break a couple. It won't necessarily be to raise money, but just for the sporting endeavour. Whether I succeed or not, time will only tell, but I'll be giving it a good go!

Many people have told me that my challenge has been an inspiration to them. Throughout this campaign I was driven by the commitment of the people who give up their time, day-in, day-out, to coach, mentor and help all the kids on the SET disability programme. I met some of the kids' parents in the disability teams, and although I'm sure they were slightly nervous of the idiot that said he was going to try and raise money for them, I hope I've earned their trust. To me, their day-to-day efforts living with the challenges that face them is awe-inspiring. If I've inspired, it's because I've been inspired.

A few weeks after last season had ended, I got a call from BBC Radio 5 Live, inviting me to the Liverpool Echo Arena for *Five Live's Big Day Out*. The presenter of *606*, Mark Chapman, said in his introduction there that over the years, the programme had phone calls that were thought-provoking and had had people talking for weeks and months afterwards. My call to them on February 23 as I travelled home from Carlisle had been that call for 2012/13.

As I walked on stage, the cheer I received was incredible. I would like to think that that cheer was not only for me, but also for every single fan of MK Dons and the wider football community that supported the project. It also further convinced me that MK Dons is not necessarily the great footballing evil that many would like to portray it as, and that I, like thousands of others, should be proud to be an MK Dons fan. And I feel we have every right to be proud.

Adam Faiers
July 2013

ABOUT THE AUTHORS

Adam Faiers lives in a small village near Milton Keynes and spends his time either cycling around the country or working to pay for bike parts. His wife Margaret has put up with his crackpot ideas for 20 years on the basis that most of them get consigned to the bin, and the ones that work are usually pretty good. They can both be found at most MK Dons games, home and away, and if you can't see them, you'll definitely hear them. Their daughter Izzie has inherited her dad's determined streak as she recently travelled around China and the Far East, mostly on her own. The Faiers are not a family to ask "Why?", but a family to say "Why not!"

Dan McCalla is an award-winning journalist who combined his writing skills and passionate support of MK Dons to help Adam create this book. Dan was named Renault MSA Young Motor Sport Journalist of the Year Award in 2011 for his World Rally Championship reporting in *Motorsport News*, but *Stadium Chase* is his first published book. Now at motoring magazine *evo*, Dan lives in Milton Keynes, where he was born and bred. He attended every MK Dons game in 2012/2013 in all competitions, both home and away, although he didn't cycle to a single one. Lazy bugger.

STADIUM CHASE

STADIUM CHASE

Printed in Great Britain
by Amazon.co.uk, Ltd.,
Marston Gate.